AN ACCIDENTAL PRUSSIAN

The Turbulent Past of a Prussian Descendant

Gabriele H. Miniter

BALBOA.PRESS

A DIVISION OF HAY HOUSE

This book is a work of non-fiction. Unless otherwise noted, the author and the publisher make no explicit guarantees as to the accuracy of the information contained in this book and in some cases, names of people and places have been altered to protect their privacy.

Balboa Press books may be ordered through booksellers or by contacting:

Balboa Press
A Division of Hay House
1663 Liberty Drive
Bloomington, IN 47403
www.balboapress.com
844-682-1282

Because of the dynamic nature of the Internet, any web addresses or links contained in this book may have changed since publication and may no longer be valid. The views expressed in this work are solely those of the author and do not necessarily reflect the views of the publisher, and the publisher hereby disclaims any responsibility for them.

The author of this book does not dispense medical advice or prescribe the use of any technique as a form of treatment for physical, emotional, or medical problems without the advice of a physician, either directly or indirectly. The intent of the author is only to offer information of a general nature to help you in your quest for emotional and spiritual well-being. In the event you use any of the information in this book for yourself, which is your constitutional right, the author and the publisher assume no responsibility for your actions.

Cover Image credit: Gabriele H. Miniter
Photo taken in the Brekke Locks near Halden, Norway

Print information available on the last page.

ISBN: 978-1-9822-6902-9 (sc)
ISBN: 978-1-9822-6901-2 (hc)
ISBN: 978-1-9822-6900-5 (e)

Library of Congress Control Number: 2021910235

Balboa Press rev. date: 06/02/2021

This book is dedicated to my husband, Sylvester, whose interest in my family history gave impetus to my writing, and to my daughter, Karen, who was always there when I needed her.

All are not taken! There are left behind
Living Beloveds, tender looks to bring
And make the daylight still a happy thing
And tender voices, to make soft the wind.

—"Consolation," Elizabeth Barrett Browning,
1806–1861

Contents

Introduction: Where Was the Kingdom of Prussia?......................xiii

Prologue: My Son Is Murdered xv

Part 1: Paternal Family Origins

Chapter 1   General Rudolf Schrader—With Whom the
            Search Began 1

Chapter 2   Jakob Heinrich von Wilm, Source of the Evidence........ 3

Chapter 3   Dr. Otto Schrader, Scholar and Nationalist.................. 7

Chapter 4   Rudolf Schrader Rises in the German Army.............. 15

Chapter 5   The Schrader Daughters 21

Chapter 6   Katharina Schrader 25

Chapter 7   Wilhelm David Walther Hesse............................... 27

Chapter 8   Moritz Hesse Converts to Christianity 29

Chapter 9   Walther Hesse Marries Katharina Schrader................. 35

Chapter 10 Wolfgang Hesse, My Father................................... 41

Chapter 11 The Hesse Family Leaves Gransee 43

Chapter 12 Life in Laasphe... 45

Chapter 13 My Father in Search of a Life............................... 47

Chapter 14 Wolfgang Meets Helga Scholze 51

Chapter 15 Wolfgang Goes to Norway.................................... 53

Chapter 16 Wolfgang Is Arrested 59

Part 2: The War Is Over

Chapter 17 My Father Finds Employment 65

Chapter 18 My Father's Life in Berleburg 69

Chapter 19 Wolfgang Takes Control of His Life 73

Chapter 20 Gabriele, the Firstborn....................................... 75

Chapter 21 Helga Gives Me Away 77
Chapter 22 My Life with Foster Parents—and Beyond 79
Chapter 23 I Am Taken Away... 89
Chapter 24 A New Home for Gabriele 93
Chapter 25 Who Will Be My New Mother?............................ 101
Chapter 26 Waltraud, Mother Number Three 103
Chapter 27 My New Family 105
Chapter 28 We Move to England....................................... 109
Chapter 29 A Detour—In Search of My "Real Mother" 119
Chapter 30 Helga Scholze, My "Real Mother" 123
Chapter 31 Frank Scholze, Helga's Brother 129

Part 3: The Tumultuous Maternal Side

Chapter 32 Paul Scholze, Political Activist............................. 133
Chapter 33 Paul Scholze, Revolutionary............................... 141
Chapter 34 Paul Scholze Becomes a Communist 147
Chapter 35 Martha Scholze... 153
Chapter 36 Paul Scholze and the IAH................................. 157
Chapter 37 The Russia Inspection 161
Chapter 38 Paul Scholze, Politician.................................... 167
Chapter 39 Paul Scholze Goes to Russia 171

Part 4: Returning to Happier Times

Chapter 40 More Memories of England................................ 181
Chapter 41 We Move to America 187
Chapter 42 I Meet My Future Husband 199
Chapter 43 Seventeen Years Later 205
Chapter 44 Life in Vermont 207
Chapter 45 I Meet My Brother, Rolf................................... 211
Chapter 46 Three Sisters Meet... 213
Chapter 47 We Move to France 215
Chapter 48 Kiawah Island, South Carolina 219
Chapter 49 We Return to France....................................... 223

Part 5: Turning Back the Clock

Chapter 50 The Extended Family 231
Chapter 51 Werner Hegemann, City Planner 233
Chapter 52 Baron Guenther von Pechmann................................ 237
Chapter 53 Baroness Alice von Pechmann, Great-Aunt 241

Introduction

Where Was the Kingdom of Prussia?

Unlike most European countries, Prussia did not have thousands of years of history to look back upon. As a "great power," it existed for only about 170 years and was "artificially" created over several centuries through the absorption and colonization of diverse smaller German and Slavic states that had been under German and Polish rule. One of these was called Prussia, a name that was then assumed for the entirety of the lands that were taken. Mostly this was done in a peaceful fashion without the imposition of or by an upper class. The integration of people occurred at all levels of society. The process brought with it not only the German language but also a more advanced civilization, as well as early Christianization. There was no basis of ethnicity or religion that originally tied them together. The country, which bordered the Baltic Sea, consisted of two colonized provinces, referred to as Eastern and Western Prussia, but over time extended to various other areas of Germany that were not geographically connected.

The capital of this new kingdom, which eventually had a king and later an emperor, was Koenigsberg, which had become a member of the Hanseatic League. Today it lies in Russia and is called Kaliningrad. To paraphrase the words of one of Germany's well-known historians, Sebastian Haffner, Prussia fought its way to become one of the great powers of Europe in the eighteenth Century ... only to find its way to a slow death. According to Haffner, it was its independent system of justice and cultural superiority, rather than its militarism which made it more dangerous to its neighboring countries. As the historian wrote in his book, *Prussia without Legend*, "as a state it arrived late on the European scene, but it sank like a meteor." The Prussian kingdom ended with the loss of World War I by Germany and the abdication of the Emperor Wilhelm II in 1918. But its final breath was not drawn until 1947 when both flight of the population and expulsion by the victors of the war brought about the dissolution of the Prussian state. No one mourned its loss as a country, yet for millions of people it was a tragedy. They lost not only their homes and possessions, but most of all, their families, and what was once a "glorious past." This book is the search for my ancestors in that abolished land. And if their genes define our personalities and our own lives, then I must also call myself a Prussian, albeit an accidental one.

Prologue

My Son Is Murdered

When the telephone rang at 8:30 a.m. on Saturday, April 18, 1992, in my home in Vermont, I could not know that this call would change my life forever. It was the Saturday before Easter. Detective A. of the West Palm Beach Police Department in Florida called to inform me that there had been an accident, and my son, Kevin, was dead. He had been murdered—shot in a senseless killing during the early hours of the morning while driving a car outside a nightclub. The car was not my son's and had been lent by a friend. Apparently, someone wanted it, the means of payment being a single bullet fired from a 'Saturday night special.'

I would like to be able to say that I do not remember much of what happened after that, but such is not the case. Memory has not eluded me here, for I very well recall pacing the length of our home back and forth for days in a state of disbelief, repeating and repeating, "No, no, no, this is not true; this did not happen." I was not riveted to the ground; instead, I was propelled into a frenzy of useless activity to do something, anything, that could change the reality of this news, to change what could not be changed.

My immediate instinct was to fly to Florida, to confront the bearer of this terrible news and the assassin. But I was persuaded that, because it was the Easter weekend, this would serve no purpose. Instead, Kevin's father as well as other family members and friends needed to be notified, a funeral home chosen, and arrangements made. My husband did it all.

He was the source of my survival. Through him, the words *love* and *support* achieved new meaning.

Kevin's body had to be shipped back to Vermont, and the Monday following that horrific Easter he arrived at the Burlington Airport at 10:00 p.m. I still remember the terrible sense of urgency to be on time for the arrival of that flight—wishing to propel the car forward, afraid and yet needing to be there.

Kevin arrived in a box, long and slender, marked "Human Remains." A luggage cart had brought it from the plane across the tarmac to the waiting hearse. I clung to it, not wanting to let go of him, as if wrapping my arms around that box could breathe life into it. After a few moments, my arms were gently removed by a friend who worked at a funeral home. My husband held me then, and we returned home.

At Kevin's funeral service a few days later, I placed one white rose on his coffin. The service was followed by a gathering of mourners in our home, during which I acted the part of a distraught but gracious hostess. It was a role for which I had few credentials and no experience. How else but through acting does one survive such an event when one's son has just been murdered? Kevin was only twenty-four years old, a loving and caring young man who had openly lived a gay life. There were no words for the despair, the sorrow, and the emptiness I felt at his loss. I just needed to keep moving.

We flew to Florida two days later to learn firsthand where Kevin's murder had occurred and to speak to the authorities. The detective who had called us was kind and optimistic that the killers would be found. The mayor of West Palm Beach assured me that no stone would be left unturned to find them, for the event had left a black mark on her city. In spite of repeated phone calls and requests for news, I never heard from either one of these individuals again. I have never learned who killed my son.

Some years before, I had become an American citizen. America had wrapped its myth of falsehoods around me, lulled me into a sense of security. It tends to do that with its promise of democracy, of freedom to live as one chooses, its system of justice that purports to exceed any other, and its Statue of Liberty with its fabled beacon of hope and safety. Never is one warned that death is as close as the nearest gun a citizen might carry, often legally, frequently not. My son had merely become another statistic in a country that tolerates such events, abhors them publicly for a brief time, and then moves on. I had willingly taken an oath of allegiance to this America because I finally wanted a home, a sense of belonging to a place, never having lived anywhere long enough before being displaced, and I wanted to vote in the country I now called my home. But America betrayed me, and I have never forgiven it.

Strangely, Kevin had a sense of foreboding that he would die young in this America. When he voiced this to a friend, who wrote to me of my son's premonition shortly after his murder, she had asked him, "What will your mother do if something happens to you?"

He quite simply replied, "My mother has had a fascinating life. She will write a book, and I will make an interesting chapter in it."

I myself had dreamed just a week before that Kevin had died. I told my husband of the dream and even documented it in a letter to my mother six weeks later. As one does with most dreams, I dismissed it, although I kept a copy of the letter. For many years I could not bring myself to look at the few belongings that remained of Kevin's short life, among which I found his friend's letter to me. The paper on which I wrote of events and my thoughts at the time of their occurrence are now yellowed with age, but the memories are still fresh. Perhaps it is the legacy Kevin has left me: because violence has repeatedly found its victims among the members of my family, I owe it to my son to tell their story.

Additionally, my new husband, Sylvester Miniter, had voiced interest in my family history, giving impetus to my research and my writing. Initially, his curiosity primarily concerned my potential appearance as I grew older. How had my mother looked in old age, and how might I resemble her at that stage of my life? And if it sounds surprising that this was a question I could not answer, nor in fact did I have any interest or curiosity about it, because I had known since I was a small child that my mother had given me away as an infant. By the time I was eight years old, I had had three mothers. The mother who gave birth to me was Helga, my father's first wife. As a newborn, I was given to Martha, who was to remain my foster mother for seven years, to be later followed by Waltraud, my father's second wife. But *mother* is as much a term of affection as it is a designation for someone who has given birth. In that sense, my foster mother was the only real mother I ever had. It was she, although no relation to me whatsoever, who nurtured, cared and loved me as if I were her own child throughout the dark years of World War II and beyond.

It is difficult to thread together one's early years, to know which are facts and which are 'told remembrances,' particularly when none of the participants of those times are still alive. But documents live beyond the lives of their creators and in recent times I have been able to corroborate my memories through many sources, giving validity to them. Frequently, I have asked myself, "Why was I not more curious as a young woman? Why did families not reveal their own histories during their lifetimes? Why do they guard secrets that, when revealed at a later date, might bring anguish to the next generation?"

Much too late in life, I confronted myself with this dilemma. It has caused me to dig into archives I had not known existed, read letters never meant for my eyes and discover siblings in distant places. In short, I have found the story of a family that I had considered to be like any other, until I learned of the far-reaching consequences of my ancestors' actions, their experiences, and their contributions to our culture, and consequently, to my own life. And on the assumption that my ancestors in some way also shaped me, my life, and my personality, I can also regard this as my story.

But writing about one's ancestors is like searching for the perfect shell or pebble on a beach—there are many, but which to choose and keep? Each one brings with it a particular memory of time and place and even has very different characteristics.

My decision as to where to begin was in fact made for me by the turbulence of the history of the twentieth century. It is among the ironies of life that one of the greatest dictators the world has ever seen would ultimately make it possible for me to discover my family's roots. It is due to one man's obsession with race—the obliteration of one, the Jewish, and the mythical creation of another, the "Aryan"—that I am able to tell my family's story. It is thanks to the Germanic, and perhaps Prussian, characteristic of thorough documentation that I have a great deal of evidence of the lives my ancestors lived.

Part 1

Paternal Family Origins

Chapter 1

General Rudolf Schrader—
With Whom the Search Began

LONG BEFORE HE was appointed Chancellor of Germany in 1933, and as early as 1919, while still living in the country of his birth, Austria, Hitler had defined Jews as a race and not a religion. He identified Jewish presence as an "alien race, a tuberculosis of the people," that "the ultimate goal must definitely be the removal of the Jews altogether."[1] His goal, and subsequent obsession, was to create a society of what he considered "pure Aryans." To a large degree, these views developed out of his belief that Germany had lost World War I in which he had fought, due to enemy—in other words, Jewish—propaganda, not because it was defeated. A strong sense of nationalism developed in the country, and Hitler became a powerful voice for it.

It is therefore not surprising that a great-uncle of mine—brother to my paternal grandmother and a career Army officer prior to Hitler's arrival on the political scene—had to document his "lineage of purity" in order to advance. Strangely, this led back to Russia and the Baltic countries—and to a 'treasure trove' of information.

A career soldier, Uncle Rudolf Schrader was a major at the end of World War I. It is said that as a young man he had found his military training difficult and as a result he later treated his troops with extreme fairness. In contrast to many other officers, after the war he remained committed to the military and became a member of the limited

100,000-man German army mandated by the Treaty of Versailles, which had been imposed on Germany by the victors. When Hitler came to power in 1933, Schrader professed his admiration for the latter's knowledge of history, and later, during the World War II, Schrader maintained a firm belief in German victory.

As a Prussian, his father had instilled in young Rudolf the strong belief that superiority of German culture and soul resided as much in the military as it did in all other aspects of German life. His father was my future great-grandfather and a professor at the University of Breslau. Together with hundreds of professors from German universities, and across all faculties, Dr. Otto Schrader had signed a Declaration by Professors of the German Reich on October 23, 1914. It declared that "so-called Prussian militarism could not be separated from German culture or the German soul." It further stated the belief that not only Germany's but also all of Europe's future was dependent on the victory of Germany's military. Assumedly, until his death in 1945, Rudolf subscribed to this conviction.

In order to remain and advance within the military, which he did rather rapidly, my great-uncle Rudolf had to present evidence of being a "pure German," that is to say, having no Jewish but rather only "pure Aryan blood." His proof of Aryan descent consisted of a certificate identifying his parents as Protestant, though formerly Greek Orthodox on his mother's side. The certificate further established that his maternal grandfather had been elevated to the nobility by Tsar Nicholas I of Russia in 1851. It was this crucial grandfather of his, my paternal great-great-grandfather, Jakob Heinrich von Wilm, who stimulated my research.

Chapter 2

Jakob Heinrich von Wilm, Source of the Evidence

JAKOB HEINRICH VON Wilm was born on July15, 1804, in Pskov, one of the oldest cities in Russia. It is located in the western part of that country, about eight miles east of the Estonian border. Its first official mention in documents dates back to AD 903. Pskov lies on the banks of the Velikaya River and was referred to as the town of purling waters. To lovers of old movies, it is perhaps best known through Sergei Eisenstein's 1938 film, *Alexander Nevsky*, which tells the story of Nevsky's recapture of the town in 1241 from the Teutonic knights who had captured it several months earlier. In the fourteenth century, German merchants who were members of the Hanseatic League had a trading post in Pskov, the League being an alliance of trading guilds that dominated trade in northern Europe.

Although the city was long considered to be a bridge towards Europe, in subsequent centuries, it lost its significance. Today it is known mainly for its well-preserved medieval walls, its Kremlin, its many small and colorful churches, as well as being the place where Alexander Pushkin wrote a number of his great works. It is here that he created his verse novel, *Eugene Onegin*, as well as the historical tragedy *Boris Godunov*. And it was in Pskov "at a railroad siding, aboard the imperial train that Tsar Nicholas II of Russia signed the Manifesto announcing his abdication as Emperor in March of 1917."[2]

There is no record of where Jakob Heinrich von Wilm attended school or university. However, by 1834 he is listed in archives as being a resident of Riga in Latvia, a city about 175 miles southwest of Pskov. Latvia had been fought over and ruled by Russia, Sweden, Poland, and Germany throughout the centuries. Its capital, Riga, had in fact been founded by Germans in AD 1201. Like Pskov in Russia, Riga became a principal port of the Hanseatic League as it lies directly on the Baltic Sea.

For centuries, Germans exercised great power over Latvia, politically, culturally, and religiously. The ruling class was constituted mainly of German nobility who owned great estates. German was one of the official languages.

However, the Russian tsar, Peter the Great, who ruled the country from 1682 to 1725, wanted to enlarge his empire and, more importantly, he wanted access to ports on the Baltic Sea. In 1710, he conquered both Estonia and Latvia. The latter country was permitted to "maintain its financial system, its administrative bodies, its Lutheran religion as well as the German language,"[3] and until the middle of the nineteenth century, Germans were the largest ethnic group in Latvia.

It was in this environment and culture in which my great-great-grandfather, Jakob Heinrich Wilm, practiced law in Riga. His career can probably best be classified as civil servant, as he held a number of titles that no longer exist today. Most significantly, he was a "Judge of the Imperial Court," a position ostensibly of some importance to the tsar. It was in this capacity that the Russian monarch bestowed on him a hereditary title, allowing him to use the *von* in his name. Thus, a man who had been born into a long line of commoners and tradesmen, such a tailors, teachers and mirror-grinders, named Wilm, was now permitted to call himself and his descendants von Wilm, the *von* being the German equivalent of the French *de* before the family name and designating nobility.

Under Peter the Great, in the eighteenth century, a reform of noble titles had taken place. This reform was enshrined in a Table of Ranks structuring the higher levels of state administrators and members of the court into fourteen classes. Henceforth, a title was not to be based merely on inheritance or wealth, but rather on accomplishment.

While at first this applied primarily to the military, revised ranking in later years, always at the direction of the tsar, was also applied to civil servants. Not only Russians but also foreigners or people of lower birth were eligible to receive titles. Because the requirements to achieve one were extremely high, in reality a title was seldom granted. Additionally, not all titles were able to be passed on to future generations. Although this system of ranking ended with the Russian Revolution in 1917, the titles already granted were allowed to remain, and thus the von Wilm family retained its aristocratic status.

Jakob Heinrich von Wilm had married twice, the first marriage to Johanna Charlotte Stieda taking place in Riga in 1831 and producing six children, two of whom died shortly after their birth. The second child, born in 1834, was Peter Nicolai von Wilm, later to become a composer and conductor of some renown. His piano pieces, his choral and chamber music, as well as his violin and cello sonatas are performed to this day. By strange coincidence, a cousin of mine, who was temporarily living in Finland in order to perfect her Finnish language skills, found copies of his musical scores in a local antique shop. Today it is possible to listen to his compositions on YouTube. At the time of the discovery of his musical scores we knew that he was a member of our family but did not know of the exact relationship. Peter Nicolai initially studied at the Leipzig Conservatory and became a music teacher at the Saint Petersburg Nikolai Institute, but later lived in Germany, both in Dresden and in Wiesbaden, where he died in 1911.

His first marriage having been dissolved in 1850, Jakob Heinrich von Wilm was married a second time, in 1852, to Alexandra von Kamienski, a member of a Lithuanian aristocratic family. She was born in Schaulen near Vilnius in Lithuania on January 1, 1830. The city lies approximately ninety miles southeast of Riga. Again, there were six children, three of each gender, assumedly all born in Riga. All the males were highly educated, one in the law, who served as a government minister, and another in philosophy; the third became a Prussian military officer. Some married into other titled families. But it was through the marriage of a von Wilm daughter to a commoner that the nobility associated with the lineage ended in relation to my immediate family.

Chapter 3

Dr. Otto Schrader, Scholar and Nationalist

MARIE VON WILM, the fourth child of the von Wilms and the first female child of the marriage of Jakob Heinrich von Wilm and Alexandra von Kamienski, was born in June of 1858. It was Marie who would later become my great-grandmother and whom I still knew as a small child. She died at the age of ninety-two in 1950 in Western Germany.

Marie married Dr. Otto Schrader, an untitled but brilliant philologist and Indo-European scholar in 1879. His seminal work, translated as *Prehistoric Antiquities of the Aryan Peoples: A Manual of Comparative Philology and the Earliest Cultures,* was first published in 1890 at the university city of Jena. Otto Schrader's work dealt primarily with the migration of the vocabulary of German and other European languages and dialects. His research centered on finding common ancestral terms in language for material things such as plants, animals, and even ordinary household items such as *table, bed,* or *chair.* Never does it imply that the word *Aryan* refers to a superior race, as it was later misused by Hitler and other extreme nationalists.

In the preface to his monumental work, my great-grandfather states the following: "As the archaeologist, armed with pick and shovel, descends into the depths of the earth, in order to trace the footsteps of the past in bone and stone remains, so the student of language might endeavor to employ the flotsam and jetsam of language—washed on the shore of history from ages immeasurably remote—to reconstruct the picture of the primeval age."

In addition to the above-mentioned work, which is still used in universities today, Schrader lectured on the origin of words and their application in various cultures and wrote hundreds of articles, although no complete list has ever been compiled. It is, however, curious that a translated copy of the work resided in the Jimmy Swaggart Bible College and Seminary Library at Baton Rouge, Louisiana. This evangelical Pentecostal religious institution is known primarily for biblical studies and certainly not for the study of the origins of language. Assumedly, it was acquired by this institution in the mistaken belief that by virtue of its title, it supported Hitler's theory that the German Aryan race was the superior and master race, with Christianity at its base. There was never any implication of an Aryan race in my great-grandfather's publications. The term *Aryan* at the time of his writing was applied only to the migration of language. In the latter nineteenth and early twentieth centuries, the meaning of the word *Aryan* was a reference to very old Indo-European languages. This translated version of my great-grandfather's book was a gift from my husband that he acquired from the above-named library.

The author, Otto Schrader, had been born into a Protestant family of civil servants on March 28, 1855, in Weimar, Thuringia. Although Weimar is today mainly associated with Germany's failed Republic of 1918–1933, it was for many years the center of German culture. Johann Wolfgang von Goethe, "poet, novelist, and playwright ... as well as actor, administrator, scientist, geologist and philosopher,"[4] made his home and spent the majority of his life here, as did Germany's beloved poet, playwright, and philosopher Johann Christoph von Schiller.

In 1919, the architect Walter Gropius founded the famous art school named Bauhaus in Weimar. It would become one of the most influential schools of the modern art movement. Its goal was to combine arts and crafts in order to create a total work of art with emphasis on the design of simple household objects. Mass production was intended to profit from this movement. Its brief life ended with the ascent of the Hitler regime, which considered it to be Jewish-influenced and therefore "degenerate."

Otto Schrader's father, Carl Nikolaus Schrader, was a senior government counselor to the Grand Duke in Weimar, holding a title that no longer exists in Germany. Loosely interpreted, it corresponded to an undersecretary of a governmental department in a German duchy. His son Otto, my future paternal great-grandfather, attended the gymnasium (high school) in Weimar. Later he studied in Jena at the Friedrich Schiller University, which had been founded in 1558, as well as in Leipzig and Berlin. In 1877, while still a student in Leipzig, Otto Schrader gave a speech entitled "Linguistics and Cultural History," thereby defining early in his academic life the direction his future research and writings would take.

Jena was then and remains not only a university city, but in the nineteenth century, it also became a world center for the optics industry, which thrives there to this day. The city was in those years the focal point of a movement calling for unification, politically and administratively, of the many German states. This transformation was brought about by Otto von Bismarck, first Chancellor of Germany, in 1871, at the end of the Franco-Prussian War. The movement was to have a strong influence on my great-grandfather Schrader. That he was a firm believer in the superiority of German, and specifically Prussian, culture is validated by his signing the "Declaration by Professors of the German Reich" in 1914.

Otto Schrader obtained his doctorate in philology, the study of languages with emphasis on their development and their relationship to cultures, in Jena in 1878. He subsequently taught at the gymnasium, which was at the time named after the grand-duke of Saxony. In addition, and most likely to supplement his income, he was a private tutor and lecturer. The following year, in 1879, he married Marie von Wilm, who was to become my great-grandmother. It was due to her marriage to Dr. Otto Schrader, a 'mere' though brilliant commoner, that the aristocratic von Wilm line came to an end in our family.

During his teaching days, which were probably not well remunerated, my great-grandfather also conducted research that led to an invitation by the dean of the faculty of philology to give a trial lecture on February 7, 1887 on his "Thoughts of the Cultural History of Indo-Europeans on a Linguistic Basis." The term *Indo-European* refers to a language family native to Eurasia that gave birth to many of the languages spoken today, all having a common ancestor. From it are derived the majority of languages spoken in Europe. Eventually, in 1890 Otto Schrader was made an *Ausserordentlicher Professor* (an untenured professor with limited internal administrative rights and functions) at the Schiller University in Jena. This title no longer exists and can perhaps be considered close to the title of adjunct professor in the American university system. No doubt, the publication of his vast encyclopedia entitled *Prehistoric Antiquities of the Aryan Peoples*, referenced above and already published and translated into English by 1890, was the reason he was finally given a professorship, albeit an untenured one.

The word *Aryan* derives from the Sanskrit term for an Indo-European people who invaded northern India around 2000 BC. Unfortunately, the word was totally misappropriated by the Hitler regime to falsely identify non-Jews in their efforts to cleanse the entire German population of its Jewish citizens. The year Schrader became a professor, 1890, was also the year Otto and Marie's son Rudolf was born. It is thanks to the documentation of his so-called 'Aryan' ancestry, which he had to provide in order to be promoted in Hitler's army, that I was able to trace my own family's roots.

To better comprehend the vast impact of Otto Schrader's work, I will quote from its preface as written in English by my great-grandfather himself, in which he refers to the subject as the birth of Linguistic Paleontology—"the study of the distant human past by linguistic means."[5]

> For some time, past, Etymology, has been a sister science to prehistoric Archaeology in the investigation of primitive culture. And now a third point of departure has been found from which to pass beyond the grounds of history. The attempt has been made by careful comparison of the antiquities of the individual Indo-European people to distinguish between what, on the one hand, they have jointly inherited in the way of manner and customs, of private, public and religious institutions, and what, on the other hand, in this

connection may be termed their recent acquisitions, whether loans from abroad or the results of their own independent evolution. Thus, to Etymology and Archaeology, a third science has been added—that of Comparative Antiquities, which, as I am firmly convinced, opens up a new prospect, full of promise, for the history of the individual Indo-European peoples. (Otto Schrader, Jena, March 1890)

Reviews and opinions of my great-grandfather's seminal work, his magnum opus, were astoundingly positive in the German press. "A work which in every respect may be described as of conspicuous excellence"; "a most remarkable book"; "one of the best works on the subject of language and antiquity published"—these were just a few of the comments written. But the book was also controversial in that Otto Schrader supported a theory proposed by an Estonian cultural historian suggesting that the Indo-Europeans were originally nomads and spoke an ancestral language native to western Eurasia, northern India, and Persia. According to this speculation, their original home was believed to have been on the steppes of eastern Europe and southern Russia. This theory was not necessarily supported by all paleontologists. In pursuit of research for his writings and his studies in Slavic languages and civilizations, my great-grandfather traveled widely, particularly throughout Russia, between 1902 and 1908.

Although the volume had been published and translated into English by 1890 to much acclaim, it apparently did not bring him the hoped-for full professorship at the University of Jena. Consequently, in 1909 Otto Schrader finally asked to be relieved of his duties there and accepted a position as full professor at the University of Breslau, approximately 280 miles to the east. It was certainly a more prestigious situation and undoubtedly brought more money into the Schrader family household.

Politically, Otto Schrader considered himself to be a National Liberal, a variant of liberalism, combining liberal policies and issues with elements of nationalism. Its goals were "the pursuit of individual and economic freedom along with national sovereignty."[6] The National Liberal Party was popular during the latter part of the nineteenth century, particularly in northern Germany. It appealed to the educated classes, especially to professors and capitalists, and had the backing of the Protestant Church. They were, from the start, firm supporters of Otto von Bismarck who served as Germany's first Chancellor after its unification in 1871, and undoubtedly this is what motivated Otto Schrader, along with many other professors, to sign the above-mentioned declaration in 1914.

My personal connection with my long-deceased great-grandfather came about in a most unusual and unexpected way. In my travels as a freelance interpreter for the American State Department in the 1990s, I accompanied a female professor of comparative political sociology from the Viadrina University, which is situated on the German border with Poland. She had been invited to tour American universities as part of the International Visitors Program sponsored by the American State Department. Having completed her own studies in Moscow, her English language skills were not as developed as her Russian. My role was to assist in her professional meetings in the United States.

To that end, we traveled together for a month to several states in America. Among other universities, she was scheduled to visit the University of Indiana at Bloomington. As part of the home hospitality phase of the program, her host, a professor of German literature, invited both of us to his residence, where he was entertaining another German female scholar. All three women, including myself, had been born in Berlin.

As we sat on the professor's terrace on a summer afternoon, enjoying a glass of wine, our conversation turned to the study of languages, their individual complexities, and their potential relationships to one another. It was in this context that I brought up the subject of my great-grandfather. I spoke about his influential work and the field of study for which he is best known, *Prehistoric Antiquities of the Aryan Peoples* and their languages. Our host enquired as to his name, and on being told Dr. Otto Schrader, the professor excused himself and seconds later returned, a thick volume in hand, obviously part of his personal library. It was my great-grandfather's book, the very volume of which we had just spoken! He generously presented it to me as a gift. Needless to say, I was extremely touched and overwhelmed. Tears came to my eyes.

In this emotional state I telephoned my husband to tell him of this unusual event. His immediate thought, on hearing my voice, was that something dreadful had befallen me.

Not only was the professor's generosity profound, but so was the coincidence. What were the possible chances that in the home of a complete stranger, at a university in the middle of America, I would find a connection to my ancestor? Strangely, this leather-bound edition had been published in 1901 in Strasbourg in the Alsace region of France. At that time, the Alsace was German, France having lost the territory to Germany following the Franco-Prussian War of 1870–71. Today it is again France, although its history remained turbulent throughout both World Wars. And stranger still, many years later my husband and I acquired a home in the Alsace in which we resided for sixteen years.

Throughout its history and since its first mapping around AD 142–147, Breslau had been controlled by many countries, including Poland, Bohemia, Hungary, Prussia, and later Germany. At the time of my great-grandfather's professorship in the Department of Indo-Germanic Philology, Breslau was in German hands. As a result of changing borders after World War II, the city again became Polish, returning to its Slavic roots, which had long existed prior to the creation of the Prussian State. Today it is known as Wroclaw.

Although I know nothing of their personal lives before Otto Schrader and Marie von Wilm married in 1879, all the papers pertaining to his professional life were generously made available to me during my visits to both Jena and Breslau universities in 2007.

Dr. Otto Schrader had a command of many languages, among them Russian and Sanskrit, and his English was of such fluency that he assisted in the proofreading as well as the writing of the above-mentioned introduction in the 1890 English translation of his work by Frank Byron Jevons. A tutor at the University of Durham in England, Jevons was himself a scholar and a lecturer in the classics. The complete translation of my great-grandfather's work is his, and as such, this accomplishment is mentioned in his own biography.

Breslau (Wroclaw) in 2007

My great-grandfather died in Breslau on March 21, 1919, at the age of sixty-four. In the family, it had been said that he died of starvation, and while the economic circumstances in Germany at the time might have supported this possibility, his obituary points to a long-lasting illness. This "son of Weimar," as he is referred to, had a "brilliant personality, was quick-witted and had a superior sense of humor." That he was a "master of the spoken and the written word" is a given considering his aptitude for languages. But, as the obituary continues, "the life of this ardent friend of the Fatherland was overshadowed, not only by his illness, but also by the collapse of power and a future" following the loss of World War I. He spent his final hours seated in an armchair in his bedroom with a view into his study. His eyes remained focused on a picture of Otto von Bismarck, who had united the many states within Germany into one nation. My great-grandfather's accomplishments and contributions in his chosen field have been honored with a bronze plaque on one of the university's buildings in Breslau.

Chapter 4

Rudolf Schrader Rises in the German Army

FROM THE BEGINNING of World War I in August 1914, food supplies in Germany were severely limited. The government, believing the war would be a short one, had made no economic plans for the population. Since Germany depended for about a third of its food requirements on imports, it severely impacted the economy when the British Navy established a blockade. It had been instigated by Winston Churchill, then First Lord of the Admiralty, who planned to starve the entire German population. As men and horses were called up to serve in the military, women had to take over the running of farms, encumbered by lack of equipment and adequate manpower. Animals lost weight due to a shortage of fodder, which in turn reduced the meat supply. In short, the country was hungry, and riots occurred in several German cities.

Otto Schrader's son, Rudolf, was of course well supplied in the military while the civilian population starved. It is estimated that over 900,000 people died of starvation during the period of the war. Extreme poverty ensued, affecting much of the population and equally impacting the Schrader family.

Dr. Otto Schrader and Marie von Wilm had four children. In addition to Rudolf, the youngest, born in 1890, there were three daughters—Else, Gertrud, and Katharina—all of whom had been born in Jena. It was Rudolf who required evidence of "genealogical purity" in order to later be promoted in Hitler's Army. Copies of documents attesting to his falsely named "Aryan Heritage," dated 1933 and 1936, support these claims. They undoubtedly enabled Uncle Rudolf's quick rise in the ranks. He had been able to confirm that among his ancestors there were no Jews.

Following his entrance into the German Army as a noncommissioned officer in 1909, Rudolf attended the War College for training and was promoted to the rank of Second Lieutenant in August of 1910. By 1912, he had been assigned to the Royal Prussian Telegraph Battalion, and at the outbreak of World War I in August 1914, he was made head of the Telegraph Unit of the First Cavalry Division. By early 1915, he had been promoted to First Lieutenant and had taken on the responsibility for complicated transmission sites. He served in Verdun in 1917, was made Captain in 1918, and was assigned to the Prussian War Ministry the same year. During World War I, he received two Iron Crosses, awarded for bravery, as well as several other decorations.

As stated earlier, he remained a member of the permitted 100,000-man army as a career soldier following the end of the war. Although the Treaty of Versailles disallowed the construction of heavy weapons, vehicles, ships, and aircraft, secret testing of weapons and undoubtedly improved methods of communication continued in Germany with the help of the Russians. By 1920, Uncle Rudolf was also a married man, although the marriage appears to have been childless. What became of his wife is not known.

During the years of Adolf Hitler's ascent to power, Rudolf Schrader also continued his rise in the German Army. By 1936, he had become a colonel, and by 1939 he was a high-level intelligence officer on the Western Front. As of June 14, 1940, he was in France, having been installed as Intelligence Commander of Paris. His first action there was the creation of a transmission site at the Arc de Triomphe, and as part of the military administration of occupied France, he became Senior Intelligence Officer. While sitting in the seat of the former head of power, he proudly sent home a telegram stating, "I am sitting at the desk of Pierre Laval," the former Prime Minister of France. Although Laval early in his career had socialist leanings and had regarded Germany as the enemy, his fortune was better served by becoming a collaborator of the Nazis, and he held a prominent position in Pétain's Vichy regime. At the end of World War II in 1945, he was convicted of treason and later executed.

On October 21, 1940, Rudolf Schrader was promoted to head all intelligence and counterespionage in France. In that capacity, he was totally responsible for transmissions, as well as security, repair, and surveillance of all French cable networks, the restoration of destroyed networks, and the personnel required for all intelligence locations in Paris, which naturally were important to the Germans, as well as for the connection between the various military administrative locations in the country. It is in no small measure due to his involvement that the Germans in France were able to deploy radio-detection cars that could track down clandestine radio signals from members of the Resistance. The majority of those caught were tortured and killed.

General Rudolf Schrader, great-uncle

Eventually, Rudolf was sent to the Eastern Front, to Russia, where he also served for several years as a high-level intelligence officer, having been promoted to Lieutenant General in 1942. He was rewarded with the German Cross in Silver, an award given for multiple distinguished services in the war effort. While in Russia, he became ill, and although he recovered and continued to serve there, it appears that he came to the realization that Germany's prospects of winning the war were not good. His mother and sister Else were still living in Breslau, in Germany's east, and were in danger as Russian troops were advancing. He telegraphed to them that they should leave for the western part of Germany immediately. Although the exact date of this telegram is unknown, it likely was sent late in 1944 as Russian troops were advancing on Breslau, a city which Hitler had commanded *must* be defended. Presumably, they left before January 19, 1945, the final date by which all remaining civilians were forced to leave.

It was a bitter cold winter, and thousands died as a result of this order. If there was ever any doubt that Rudolf Schrader had functioned within the highest circles of Hitler's regime, this telegram was perhaps the best proof. No one outside the inner circle could have known how precarious Germany's position was or how quickly the enemy was approaching. Rudolf, having served in Russia himself until 1944, was now assigned to the Fuehrer Reserve, a group of high-level reserve officers in the German Army, who were waiting to be reassigned to new positions. As late as April 1945, he was awarded one of the highest German medals, given to only 100 people throughout the entire war, the War Merit Cross with Swords. This award, specifically "with swords" was given to soldiers for exceptional service "not in direct connection with combat."[7]

When Germany capitulated to the Western Allied troops in 1945, Rudolf Schrader became an American prisoner of war and was brought to what had now become the American Military Hospital at Wiesloch, near Heidelberg. Since 1933 a clinic in this small town had been charged with the sterilization of humans and children's euthanasia. It had also been a general point of deportation to concentration camps. For Rudolf, it became a prison, and by August 1945, he was dead. My father later stated that it is unknown whether his uncle Rudolf committed suicide or was shot in attempting to escape. Official documents claim that he committed suicide on August 22, 1945. I have visited the gravesite containing his ashes in the small military cemetery located adjacent to the clinic. The grave is marked with the number 75.

His suicide has been questioned. Some have speculated that he died at the hands of his American captors, particularly since many of his medals have appeared on collectors' sites on the Internet in recent years. My personal belief, with no evidence to the contrary, is that suicide was, for a man of his class and convictions, the most likely if not the most honorable path to take. He was a Prussian soldier through and through, blinded by his devotion to a system, a country, and a Fuehrer who had led Germany into an abyss. He had been an important participant in the destruction of the very culture and principles that he, his father, the country's educated class, and his Protestantism had so highly valued. I do not believe he could have lived with himself or ever again faced his family, especially in light of the fact that one of his sisters had married a "half Jew." All his proof of "Aryan descent" had led only to mass murder and created a world of chaos. The consequences caused the world to change forever.

Chapter 5

The Schrader Daughters

I DO NOT know the birth order of Otto Schrader and Marie von Wilm's remaining three children, the daughters Else, Gertrud, and Katharina. Else became a schoolteacher who in later years awakened in me the great pleasure of reading. When I was a small child, Else was always suspect and a little frightening. She had lost the vision of an eye as a result of a tennis accident as a young woman and wore a patch over the "sightless cavity." She had married Richard Schoch, who became President of the Senate, equivalent to chairman of a high civilian court, in Breslau. He was strongly anti-Nazi, had a love of music and history, and died on the streets of Breslau of a heart attack during the war years. Their only child, a son named Horst, was also musically inclined and became an orchestra conductor of modest success in spite of the fact that he was married to the niece of Wilhelm Furtwaengler, one of Germany's greatest conductors and a devoted Nazi. (My husband, the scientist, always jokingly referred to Horst as a "semiconductor.") It was to Else, Rudolf's sister, and to his mother, Marie (von Wilm) Schrader, who were still living in Breslau, that Rudolf had sent the urgent telegram in the last days of the war, advising them to flee to the west.

A second daughter, Gertrud, had married Eberhard Greiner who headed the art department of a porcelain manufacturing company in Maastricht, Holland. Sharply critical of the German National Socialist

(Nazi) Party, he was nevertheless a party member, an incongruity that eventually caused him to be dismissed by the Dutch company once they became aware of it. His entire family were strong adherents of the philosophical system known as Anthroposophy, which held a belief in human wisdom as opposed to Theosophy or divine wisdom. It was an esoteric movement founded by Rudolf Steiner in the early twentieth century. Some believed it to be "the most important esoteric society in European History";[8] others have criticized it as being pseudoscientific. The philosophy speaks not only of the reincarnation of the human spirit, but also of the belief that after death the human spirit reviews the past life, resulting in rebirth in a body and parents of one's choosing.

There are a number of practical fields in which Anthroposophy is applied even today. The Waldorf Schools are an example. Founded in Stuttgart, Germany, in 1919, they operate on the principle that "children's creative, spiritual and moral dimensions need as much attention as their intellectual ones."[9] The first schools were founded for workers of the Waldorf-Astoria cigarette factory workers, hence the name. Steiner recognized the importance of developing the "whole person which included teaching artistic and practical skills as well as social skills and spiritual values."[10] Today these schools can be found all over the world. Steiner's ideas were also influential in the field of agriculture, and he is considered to be among the founders of today's organic farming movement. The 'Alternative Medical Movement' is also attributed to him and has led to its application by hundreds of doctors throughout the world. As an architect, Steiner designed numerous buildings, including those of the organizational headquarters of the movement that survive and are today still located in Switzerland. Many institutions, including banks, charities and businesses, implement Steiner's concepts which are "aimed at harmonious and socially responsible roles in the world economy."[11] According to Harvard Business School historian Geoffrey Jones, Steiner and fellow adherents of his philosophy had "considerable impact on the creation of many businesses in organic food, ecological architecture and sustainable finance."[12]

Rudolf Steiner was neither Jewish nor a nationalist. The Anthroposophy movement, in fact, had few National Socialist members, although they had many adherents among the world's intellectuals.

Steiner lectured often on Judaism, seeing no need for it to exist as a religion or a culture and argued for its assimilation into society as a whole. He wished Anthroposophy to be free of any religious denomination and considered blood, race and folk as primitive instincts. While he was a fierce opponent of anti-Semitism, he "saw the Jews completely integrating into the larger society."[13]

By the time the Nazis assumed power, Steiner was no longer alive, having died in 1925. The movement continued to exist, however, and although banned during Hitler's time, it even had some secret Nazi adherents. Among them was Rudolf Hess, a leading member of the Nazi Party and Hitler's deputy. Hitler considered Anthroposophy to be "Jewish methods" and sent a number of followers of this philosophy to concentration camps.

After the war, due to Gertrud Schrader's husband Eberhard Greiner's connection to the Nazi Party, he was also dismissed from a subsequent job with a West German steel company. The family fell on hard times financially, in the end becoming dependent on the support of the State. Gertrud died of a heart attack in a retirement home of the Anthroposophy movement in Germany. I never met this great-aunt of mine and have no knowledge of what became of her husband.

Chapter 6

Katharina Schrader

KATHARINA, MY PATERNAL grandmother and the Schraders' third daughter, was born in Jena, Thuringia, in 1882. Sadly, I know nothing of her childhood. Aside from personal memories as my grandmother, a sweet reminder of her youth is an autograph album, which I inherited. At the time of her childhood, it was fashionable for young girls to have such albums in which friends would write sentimental messages or poems dedicated to each other. Katharina, or Kaethe, as she was known throughout her life, had begun such an album on February 11, 1891, the last dated entry being January 26, 1894. At that time, Kaethe would have been twelve years old. It is charming evidence of another era, a time lived more slowly, a time to reflect on friendships.

By any standards, Kaethe was a beautiful young woman. Tall and slim, with a lovely face above a long and slender neck, she gazes seriously into the camera in a photograph taken in 1907, three years before her marriage. Many photographs of her early years exist, but I am particularly fond of an enlarged version of this one, which adorns the walls in our home. The image exudes warmth, a feeling I was to experience firsthand from her in later years.

All I know of the Schrader family's life is that financially they were not well-to-do. No doubt, four children strained the income of a university professor, no matter how accomplished or brilliant his research and publications. A story was told in our family that Kaethe had received an invitation to a ball by a young man of some social standing and of whom she apparently was fond. Because there was no money to buy a suitable ballgown, she could not accept his invitation.

How she met her future husband, my grandfather Walther Hesse, I do not know, although it is likely they met in Jena. Kaethe's father, Otto Schrader, was at that time still a professor at the University of Jena, and Walther a student of the law. Their engagement lasted several years, but on November 27, 1910, she married Walther Hesse, attorney and notary in the European sense of that legal specialty, in Breslau. Kaethe was twenty-eight years old, an advanced age at that time for a young woman to marry.

Katharina Schrader, my paternal grandmother, 1907

Chapter 7

Wilhelm David Walther Hesse

MY PATERNAL GRANDFATHER was known all his life only by the name Walther. Born in 1881 in Triebel, which today lies in Poland, he was of Jewish origin, his father, Moritz Hesse, having been born into that faith. This was a fact that my grandmother apparently only discovered, much to her dismay, at some belated point after her engagement to Walther. Although an emancipation law, passed in 1869, had eliminated all restrictions previously imposed on people of different faiths, thereby creating equality under the law for all Jews, in everyday life this was not observed. Since in the early part of the twentieth century Jews constituted less than 1 percent of Germany's population, perhaps Walther thought it unnecessary, or even inadvisable, to disclose the fact of his parentage to the daughter of an ardent nationalist.

Chapter 8

Moritz Hesse Converts to Christianity

WALTHER'S FATHER, MY great-grandfather Moritz Hesse, was born on July 20, 1850, in Rybnik in the region of Pomerania, which lies on the southern shore of the Baltic Sea and was at the time part of Prussia. Following World War II these lands were divided between Germany and Poland. Moritz had been named after his maternal grandfather, Moritz Hoeniger. His own parents, Wilhelm Hesse and Friederike Hoeniger, both of the Jewish faith, had owned a distillery in Rybnik.

Although Moritz was certainly born a Jew, in genealogical records of the family only one son, Josef, born to them in 1851, one year after Moritz, is identified. It is assumed that Moritz was disinherited or, at a minimum, deliberately taken out of the family line, as a result of his religious conversion to the Reformed Christian Church. It was not uncommon for such expulsion to occur. What is not known is whether Moritz's conversion came about due to religious conviction or his wish to marry Maria Louise Ernestine Pesch, born in 1855 in Berlin. She was the Christian daughter of a well-to-do businessman whose family originally came from Galicia in Spain.

Neither of Moritz's parents were present at their civil wedding ceremony. It was attended by only two witnesses, one being his uncle David, his father's brother, who had also acted as witness at the wedding of Moritz's brother Josef. According to my father, who lived with his grandparents, Moritz and Maria, while attending the gymnasium in Brandenburg, Moritz never spoke of his Jewish roots, and perhaps it was not on his son Walther's mind either at the time of his engagement to Kaethe Schrader.

Maria Pesch, my paternal great-grandmother, entered the Hesse family preceded by an unusual reputation. There were claims that Maria previously had a bankrupt lover and that my great-grandfather, Moritz, her future husband, paid off his debts. Why he would have done this remains a mystery, although it does add some color to the family history.

There are no records as to where Moritz Hesse studied law. He originally practiced his profession as a magistrate in the small town of Triebel, which was at that time also part of Prussia. Today this small community lies in Poland. By the time of his marriage to Maria Pesch in 1879, he held the title of Royal District Judge, a highly respected position in the town of Brandenburg, which lies west of Berlin. The city, once known as Brennabor, dates back to the seventh century. It had also been a member of the Hanseatic League and was once a rich trading town, located on the River Havel, a tributary of one of central Europe's major rivers, the Elbe. Today it is a relatively small and picturesque city, having survived heavy destruction during World War II, followed by neglect during the Communist era. A visit in the summer 2018, almost thirty years after reunification of East and West Germany, proved that a great deal of modernization would still be required to restore it to its standing in earlier times, "the original nucleus of the former States of Brandenburg and Prussia."[14] My father wrote in later years that his grandfather Moritz had been a highly educated man, serious, moral, ethical, and kind, best demonstrated perhaps by his relieving his wife's former lover of his debts.

In addition to his legal duties, my great-grandfather wrote several books on various aspects of the law, and later developed a method of self-teaching shorthand. Although his mention in German encyclopedias includes that accomplishment, the shorthand was never widely accepted as a useful tool in Germany. The *Lexicon of German Ortho-Stenography—8 Hours of Stenography Lessons* was published in 1903 in Leipzig. In his preface to the book, my great-grandfather wrote that the "German Fatherland" should take the initiative in teaching this time-saving method to all people and cultures as "stenography saves time and time is money." He believed that his "invention could help alleviate economic battles in world markets"—a lofty goal with a modest ending. His book, however, is still available as a historic reprint.

Moritz and Maria Hesse, paternal great-grandparents

During the latter years of his life, Moritz Hesse developed an interest in socialist ideas and ideals and was in contact with Karl Kautsky, a nineteenth-century Czech-Austrian philosopher and journalist and one of the most prominent promoters of Marxism. Residing in London, Kautsky was both friend and secretary to Friedrich Engels, who was himself a philosopher, co-authoring *The Communist Manifesto* with Karl Marx and later helping finance the writing of *Das Kapital*. At the end of his life, it appears that my great-grandfather reverted to his religious roots, as he lived out his days in a Jewish retirement home where he mercifully died in 1934, before the implementation of Hitler's most brutal measures against the Jews.

Moritz Hesse, paternal great-grandfather, ca. 1933

The Christian, and ostensibly shunned side of the Hesse marriage, was my great-grandmother, Maria Louise Ernestine Pesch, born on May 8, 1855, in Berlin. Her father, Rudolf David Wilhelm Pesch, had been born in Berlin in 1820, and although a resident of that city all his life, he was a widely traveled businessman. His passport, a copy of which I possess, is a large, impressive, and quite beautiful document, complete with visas permitting travel to Switzerland, Belgium, Holland, and France. It was issued in the name of Frederick Wilhelm IV, King of Prussia, on March 27, 1841, and was signed by the minister of the interior. The passport states that it had to be presented at each location at which the bearer intended to spend more than twenty-four hours, and therefore had much the same function as passports do today. What prompted these travels, what business he was involved in, is not known. There is no reference in the family history as to why Maria's apparently wealthy father did not pay off her bankrupt lover. Could a possible scandal have ensued? Did her former lover threaten her? Mysteries such as these are best left to the imagination as there are no explanations in the family records.

Moritz, who was now no longer considered a Jew, and his Christian wife Maria had two children, Walther and Alice, born one year apart. Walther, the firstborn in 1881, later became my paternal grandfather. The birth of both children took place in the same town as their father's, in Triebel. Following in his father's footsteps, Walther studied law, not only in Jena, as mentioned earlier, but also at the University of Halle, one of the oldest universities in Germany.

As a member of the Hanseatic League, Halle had become a center for the Protestant Reformation led by Martin Luther. Beginning in the seventeenth century, it also became a breeding ground of Pietism, a movement within Lutheranism that strongly impacted Prussian culture and religion. This movement, with its emphasis on individual faith and the living of a pure Christian life, has influenced most western countries in some fashion and in particular has contributed to American evangelism.

It is impossible to say to what degree these cultural values might have affected a young man of semi-Jewish background, but I can say with certainty that my grandfather, Walther Hesse, was a Prussian to the core. There are certain "virtues" ascribed to Prussians, virtues that have been passed down through the centuries and are implanted in us, and those who are raised with them are puzzled by those who are not. Among them are the stereotypically referenced efficiency, austerity, discipline, and a strong sense of duty. It seems that these traits do not respect religious differences.

Maria Hesse with children Walther, paternal grandfather, and Alice, great-aunt

Chapter 9

Walther Hesse Marries Katharina Schrader

BY 1910, WALTHER Hesse had established a private practice as lawyer and notary, the latter a highly specialized aspect of German law, which includes property, corporate and family law as well as estate planning. It has no relationship to the American definition of a notary. Walther had settled in the small and charming town of Gransee, about thirty-five miles west of Berlin in the state of Brandenburg. Within the borders of this state lies a midsized city bearing the same name as the state, in which Walther's father Moritz had practiced law and served as a judge. The year 1910 was also when Walther married Katharina (Kaethe) Schrader, my grandmother, who had apparently overcome her dismay at learning of his Jewish origins. In light of her father's financial circumstances, one might also conjecture that it was a marriage of convenience, as Kaethe was at that time at an advanced age to be married.

Walther and Katharina Hesse, paternal grandparents, ca. 1910

Katharina, right, with her sister-in-law Alice

Katharina with her father, Otto Schrader, 1915

The coming decade could not have been a more inauspicious one to begin a family. All three of the Hesse children were born within it, beginning with my father, Alexander Woldemar Wolfgang in 1911.

Three years later came the birth of his sister Gerda in 1914, followed by Anneliese in 1916. All were born in Gransee; and all were christened in the Protestant Church of St. Marien, built in the thirteenth century, where their Protestant baptismal records reside. The three children were all confirmed into the Protestant faith in the same church, my father's confirmation taking place on April 10, 1927. Only my grandmother Kaethe continued to practice her faith for the rest of her life.

By all indications, my grandfather's law practice was a successful one. The generous family home, architecturally conceived in 1926 as a row house in the manner of the region and the times, still stands today fronting the town square. The architectural plans for his home are in my possession. The initials *WH* (Walther Hesse), surrounded by the scales of justice, still proudly adorn the archway leading to the property. A formal family photograph, probably dating to 1930, shows the interior elegantly furnished, its occupants dressed in a manner suggesting prosperity. My grandfather is seen in profile, one arm elegantly draped on a heavily carved piece of furniture. Wolfgang, my father, approximately nineteen years old at the time, looks dolefully into the camera, while the rest of the family regard the photographer with almost an air of resignation.

The Hesse Family in Gransee, left to right, Katharina, Wolfgang, Anneliese, Gerda, and Walther ca. 1930

The location of the property was an indication of my grandfather's position and affluence. The house directly faced a historic monument built by one of Germany's most prominent architects, city planners, and painters of the time, Karl Friedrich Schinkel. While the majority of his buildings can be found in the Berlin area, this particular rather grand and Gothic-inspired structure in Gransee honors the spot on which the sarcophagus of the very young and beloved Queen Louise of Prussia rested for the night of July 25, 1810, as her body was being transported to Berlin for burial. She had died at the young age of thirty-four of pneumonia, having already borne nine children. Through her father's sister Charlotte, who had married King George III of England, thereby becoming Queen of England, Louise was related to the British royal house. A city in America, in the state of North Carolina, has been named Charlotte in the English queen's honor, despite Britain's loss of many of its colonies in the American War of Independence. Even the North Carolina county of Mecklenburg is named after Queen Charlotte's ancestral home in northern Germany.

In German history, the young Queen Louise is best remembered for her unsuccessful negotiations with Napoleon Bonaparte, following Prussia's losses against the French at the Battle of Jena in 1806. In the humiliating Treaty of Tilsit, which followed in 1807, the Prussian King Frederick Wilhelm III was forced to cede half of Prussia's eastern territory and accept French occupation. In spite of charming the emperor, Louise was unable to persuade Napoleon to renegotiate these terms.

On hearing of Louise's death in 1810, Napoleon is said to have remarked to her husband that he had lost his best minister. Tourists still come today to pay their respects, and books continue to be written recounting this young queen's brief life and influence. My grandfather's house is always visible in photographs taken of this unusual monument. Following World War II, and during the Communist era, the former family home of my Hesse grandparents served for some time as the City Hall of Gransee.

Chapter 10

Wolfgang Hesse, My Father

ALTHOUGH CHRISTENED WITH the names Alexander Woldemar Wolfgang, my father was known all his life only as Wolfgang. Undoubtedly, he was given the first two names to honor ancestors, as both names appear in his mother's family line. I am aware of his full name as the result of finding an early report card.

Wolfgang was never a healthy child, plagued by asthma from the earliest. He was not athletically inclined, nor, judging by his school records, was he a particularly good student. His elementary school days were spent in the town of his birth, Gransee, but in 1923, at the age of twelve, he was sent to live with his paternal grandparents, Moritz and Maria Hesse, in the larger city of Brandenburg, in order to attend the gymnasium, as none existed in his hometown. His grandfather was by this time retired from his profession as judge.

When reflecting on the time he spent living with his grandparents, my father never alluded to his schooling, but spoke of his grandfather in the most affectionate terms, as a serious but friendly, highly educated, and respected judge. No words have survived as to how he felt about his grandmother, Maria Pesch. From other family sources I have learned that she was a severe taskmaster, making her children sleep on wooden boards without a mattress and allowing them to eat only stale, dried bread, as this was better for their teeth! Perhaps such strictures did not apply to her "sickly" grandson Wolfgang, as there is no mention by him of such treatment. His most vivid memory of her was the breast cancer operation she endured, which was performed on the dining room table by "a very unpleasant doctor." She died soon after this procedure.

Religion was not a subject ever discussed in my family. I did not grow up with the knowledge that there were many different faiths or belief systems in the world, and I do not recall when I first heard the word *Jew*, let alone its implications, before I was almost adult. As a result, it was not until relatively late in my life that my father told me there had been a large branch of the Jewish Hesse family, never spoken about, which had wanted no contact with the converted branch. By the end of World War II, they had disappeared. Although Hitler's policies did not leave the lives of my family untouched, it is perhaps due to my great-grandfather's love for a Christian woman of Spanish descent that my "half-Jewish" grandfather and my "one-quarter Jewish" father survived the hell created by the Nazi regime at all.

Survival is, however, relative. Many people were deprived of a meaningful future or existence as a result of policies enacted under the dictatorship of Adolf Hitler. My father's family is just one such example.

Chapter 11

The Hesse Family Leaves Gransee

DUE TO PERSONAL and apparently "unfortunate" circumstances, my grandfather, Walther Hesse, moved his family—wife Kaethe, son Wolfgang, and two daughters, Gerda and Anneliese—to a small town of less than ten thousand souls, very distant from Gransee and the nearby excitement of Berlin. He exchanged his law practice with that of another lawyer. What those unfortunate circumstances were, I never officially learned, although there were implications of his involvement with another woman prior to this sudden move.

Their eldest daughter Gerda, my aunt, told me many years later that on returning home from school one day, she had found her mother in tears. Apparently, Walther had announced that he planned to leave his wife and family. Gerda never forgot this or forgave her father and claimed she never respected him after that. Whatever the circumstances were, in 1931 my grandfather exchanged his legal practice with that of another lawyer and moved the family to the town of Laasphe.

This small community, lying in the province of Westphalia, was at the time still part of Prussia and remained so until 1946. It lay far to the southwest of the state of Brandenburg where Gransee was located. No one wanted to move, and his family resented it deeply. They had no wish to give up their lovely home, friends, school, and staff, only to move into an apartment over a grocery store. Gone was the familiar flat landscape with its many lakes and rivers and endless treelined avenues. By contrast, Laasphe, today a spa town and renamed Bad (Bath) Laasphe, was nestled among low-lying mountains with no wide rivers or lakes in sight. Nor was it located anywhere near a large city, such as Berlin and its excitement. The population seemingly consisted of extremely pious Lutherans. They were not welcomed any more than they wished to be there.

Everyone was unhappy about the move and still spoke of it many years later. However, *it saved their lives.* My grandfather's replacement in Gransee, a Jewish lawyer by the name of Meyer, died in a concentration camp. The family learned that Attorney Meyer had been forced to sell the house to a high-ranking Nazi, presumably at an extremely low price. Such was the custom, as property was expropriated by the Nazis. But the Hesse family lived, although in reduced circumstances. The children all completed their *Abitur*, the final gymnasium exams, in this new environment, my father doing so in February 1933. However, survival did not preclude discrimination and humiliation by the anti-Semitic population of the entire region where my grandfather and his family had now settled.

Chapter 12

Life in Laasphe

AS THE NAZIS' influence increased with Hitler's rise to power in the early 1930s, so did their stranglehold on those they considered to be less than human, among them the Jews. According to their definition of a Jew, conversion to Christianity was meaningless. Nor was it significant that one parent was "Aryan," according to the Nazi interpretation of this word. As a result, my grandfather, and later my father, were considered to be "full-blooded Jews" or, at best, "of mixed blood" and treated accordingly. Not only were their professional lives affected, but higher education was denied.

By 1935 my grandfather, who had left behind a fully established legal practice in Gransee, had joined the law office of a local attorney in Laasphe but was no longer permitted to plead cases before a higher court in a nearby city and was boycotted in the town. This small, predominantly Protestant Lutheran place was openly and abusively hostile and anti-Semitic. Following my grandfather's legal defense of a Jew in a civil case, a local citizen caused a fifteen-meter-long banner bearing the words "Don't go to Jewish lawyers" to be affixed near my grandfather's office. Prior to this event, the same individual had already defamed my grandfather in a local newspaper, accusing him of having defended a "slimy Jew" and denouncing him as a traitor who had committed a severe crime by defending this Jewish citizen.

"A pure-blooded, untainted German lawyer would have respected his inner voice as a warning and declined this mandate," he stated.

The only people who, it seemed, had the right to reside in this town were those who "carried the pure blood of our fathers."[15] The accuser had been a teacher who, at the end of the war, was dismissed and briefly imprisoned. Three years later, having survived the denazification process, he was reinstalled in his teaching position. Local political groups described him as having always been "decent," never having attempted to influence his students and very early having distanced himself from the Nazi regime. My grandfather's voice, alone and unheard in this social and political wilderness, was the only one who protested this decision, identifying this man as having been one of the strongest supporters of the Nazis.

Following the war, the tables turned, and hypocrisy was the order of the day. Suddenly no one had been an anti-Semite. My grandfather became a prominent attorney with a reputation that extended far beyond the town and counties where he lived and practiced. In 1945, he became a State's attorney and a prosecutor at the High Court of Siegen, where he had previously been barred from prosecuting cases. He became a beloved and much-admired member of the town council and was made mayor of Laasphe in 1946, a position he held for three years. He was involved and influential in community projects to create much-needed postwar housing.

Walter Hesse became a founding member, both at the local as well as at the national level, of the Christian Democratic Union, the centrist political party now known as the CDU. It is a major political party to this day and is headed by Germany's chancellor, Angela Merkel. For his commitment to the law and for his social engagement, my grandfather was awarded the Order of Merit, First Class, of the Federal Republic of Germany, which had been instituted by the first president of the Federal Republic of Germany, Theodor Heuss, after World War II.

Walther Hesse died in 1968. His obituary stated that his name and his work would continue to live on in Laasphe, this small city on the River Lahn, where he had initially been so much abused. In the male line of my family, he was replaced by the birth of my own son, Kevin, born in January of that year, far away in America.

Chapter 13

My Father in Search of a Life

THE GENERATIONAL DIVIDE in the Hesse family during the early years of the twentieth century is best demonstrated by the lack of education. Those such as my grandfather, who had survived in spite of being considered Jewish, were of an age at which they could perhaps regain position and societal status by continuing in a career that had been brutally interrupted. For my father, it was a very different story.

Wolfgang had never been a very good student, partially perhaps due to his many health problems as a child. As mentioned, he was not a particularly strong boy, not in the least athletically inclined, and all his life continued to be plagued by asthma. The only subject in which he truly excelled in school was foreign languages, and on them he was forced to base his entire future. In effect, due to the times, he was thrown onto a political and economic waste heap from which he could never fully raise himself. It affected not only his social standing but, in more ways than anyone could imagine at the time, his life and that of his children.

My father had been as much discriminated against as had his father, and certainly with more severe consequences. Following the completion of his Abitur, he was now ready for university. Although wishing to follow the family tradition of the law, he was not permitted to attend an institution of higher learning. Neither of his sisters were allowed to receive an advanced education. Since by 1936 my father was primarily living in Berlin, it must have been during a visit to his parents in Laasphe during that year that Wolfgang was paraded through the town, handcuffed and forced to wear a sign stating he was a "Race Defiler," including the legend "I have violated an Aryan woman."[16] He had been denounced to the local authorities by a resident of the town who had observed his meeting with a young local woman.

Memories of my father are of a dual nature, filled with a great deal of love but also much sorrow. He had been born into a world, a culture, and a generation dominated by tyrants. The ebb and flow of his life were determined by these factors. Following completion of his Abitur in his new home in 1933, he was only permitted to attend two semesters at language institutes, first in the city of Mannheim and then in Heidelberg, followed by a brief time in London to perfect his English skills. Additionally, a short Spanish language course at the Berlitz School in Frankfurt gave him rudimentary skills in that language.

From October 1934 until March 1935, he attended a private business school in Frankfurt. His father could afford no more, due to the discrimination he was himself suffering in his own profession. Because these were the only institutions of higher learning that admitted students of "mixed race," they were the only accomplishments my father could offer as he began his adult life. Additionally, these permitted courses were limited in their scope. They ensured that he could never achieve a level of proficiency in any specific professional field, such as language applicable to medicine, business, or the law, which might have enabled him to be promoted to some higher position. By design and by law, he had little hope of advancement.

Deciding to leave the parental home in Laasphe permanently behind following completion of his language courses, Wolfgang returned to Berlin where he hoped that career opportunities would be greater than in this sleepy little town. But even in Berlin every conceivable barrier, such as his lack of education, his supposed race and religion, and his unwillingness to support the regime or join the National Socialist Party, stood in his way.

In view of Wolfgang's inability to find employment in Germany, not even on a volunteer basis, leaving the country seemed to be the only viable path. A friend with connections had been offered passage to Brazil both for himself and for my father. Unfortunately, this offer was later rescinded. Having no resources of his own to pay either for his passage or for the security deposits required by the Brazilian government, my father discarded the plan. However, in preparation for such potential emigration, Wolfgang had determined that he needed a practical skill, and therefore completed two soldering courses. He received the certificates of completion in December 1936 and February 1937. In the event, he was forced to remain in Berlin but was later able to put these skills to some practical use.

Eventually, his limited achievements, and particularly his fluent command of both English and French, provided him employment with several small companies doing business overseas. All these positions were of brief duration and in short order he was released from one after another. Among my many family documents are eight letters of recommendation, dated between 1937 and 1940, all praising my father's work ethic and skills, while at the same time dismissing him, as the pressure to rid the country of "Jewish blood" increased. The war was given as a reason. "You are of mixed race" was implied. Wolfgang lost many valuable years of his life, years in which under normal circumstances, he could have completed the desired law degree. For purposes of education and employment, even a "mixed blood" person was considered to be a full-blooded Jew. There was no hope for any kind of economic future in Germany.

The turning point in my father's "career" as well as in his personal life came in March 1940 when a large construction company, H. Klammt, hired him, over the objections of the Gestapo, as assistant to the chief executive of their headquarters in Berlin. As the war had begun a few months earlier, in September 1939, and there was, consequently, a shortage of qualified men who had not been inducted into the army, the company prevailed in keeping Wolfgang as their employee, even at the risk of doing so illegally. My father was twenty-nine years old at this time.

Chapter 14

Wolfgang Meets Helga Scholze

IT WAS DURING the early months of this new employment at H. Klammt that my father met Helga Scholze, likewise an employee, who was to become my mother. Perhaps no two people were ever more mismatched in marriage than my parents. Ten years apart in age, frowned upon by my father's family, a free spirit and coming from totally disparate social and economic backgrounds, the marriage was doomed from the start. The fact that Helga's father was an ardent and extremely active Communist probably did not engender favor in the Hesse family either.

It may have been a chance encounter, perhaps a brief affair, but there was only one reason for the marriage to have occurred at all, and that was that I was on the way. On meeting Helga Scholze for the first time, my father's sister, Gerda, noticed that Helga had a stain on her blouse, symbolic perhaps, in Gerda's eyes, of the stain being perpetrated on the entire family. But in the 1940s, an honorable man married the unfortunate, pregnant woman, and on the assumption that Wolfgang did not want to shame either her or his family, Wolfgang married Helga on May 15, 1941, in a civil ceremony in Berlin, Charlottenburg. My birth occurred in October of that year. The "Accidental Prussian" had arrived!

Circumstances, both professional and personal, created opportunities for an almost immediate separation between the newlyweds, as my father was sent to Norway by his employer in August 1942. Although the marriage was short-lived, both eventually going their separate ways, they were joined forever through acts of betrayal and lies on Helga's part, but perhaps above all, by the fact of my existence.

Helga Scholze, my mother, ca.1941

Chapter 15

Wolfgang Goes to Norway

SINCE THE INVASION of Norway by the German Army on April 9, 1940, my father's employer, H. Klammt, had been building fortifications in various locations of that country, operating under the direction of the parent organization, Todt. The latter was both a civil and military engineering company, founded by the strangely and ominously named Fritz Todt, whose name implied "death," in this instance, both literally and figuratively. Todt, in his capacity as inspector general for German roadways, had been responsible for the construction of the German autobahn system for which Germany is still so well known today. During the Hitler era, he became Minister for Armaments and Ammunition; as a result, he was in charge of the entire German wartime military economy. Hitler gave Todt the responsibility for large engineering projects in occupied territories, and the company was notorious for its use of forced labor. Among other projects, they were responsible for the building of Nazi concentration camps.

The firm of H. Klammt sent Wolfgang to their facility in Kristiansand on Norway's southern shore. My father was never in the German military himself, but in this position was now in their service in a civilian capacity. He had proven himself to be proficient while being trained in the Berlin headquarters of the company, and management seemed willing to risk defying the Gestapo, which had disallowed the issuance of a passport for Wolfgang.

For my father, this became "the best of times and the worst of times," to quote Charles Dickens's opening of *A Tale of Two Cities*. It was in Norway that my father met the love of his life, Vivian Olaussen, setting off a chain of events that are being lived out to this day. His correspondence with Vivi while in the country, but particularly after his forced departure, is the basis for my understanding of that period of his life.

Wolfgang Hesse was made head of purchasing for the H. Klammt firm in Kristiansand. In that role, he was responsible for all inbound and outbound shipping of war materials and supplies. His duties required considerable travel within Norway, a country with which he quickly fell in love, and whose language he easily conquered. For the rest of his life, my father received Norwegian newspapers in our home, and a Norwegian dictionary was forever at his side.

Travel and meetings in parts of Norway distant from Kristiansand were sometimes of several days' duration, and often Stavanger and Lillehammer were among Wolfgang's destinations. He writes of encounters with individuals, some of whom were of dubious character and were obviously collaborating with the Germans in some capacity. One man did not appear for the designated meeting, and my father wrote that a bad reputation had preceded this man, that he treated his wife like a dog, was a drunk, and slept everywhere except at home! Lillehammer in particular impressed him with its seven-hundred-meter-long, "new grey-green bridge over emerald waters, the most wonderful thing I have ever seen," he wrote, "the red and blue evening sky and its many hills, straight streets in which not a single house could be called unattractive." It was here Wolfgang wanted to take Vivi on their honeymoon.

All his life, my father was affected by the beauty of physical landscapes, and with real delight his letters describe the pleasure these travels through the Norwegian countryside gave him. He was always an approachable and charming human being, and so, undoubtedly, conversed with his fellow voyagers. One letter relates that passengers in the same train compartment in which he was traveling thought that he was Indian due to his rather dark complexion.

He always admired what he considered to be the "decent, kind and humanitarian" behavior of the Norwegians, in contrast to what he had experienced in Nazi Germany. He wrote about an older woman, who, on one of his train trips, offered him cherries from the large supply she was carrying in a basket. He mentioned a gentleman traveler who was bemoaning the lack of cigarette papers, commonly used to roll one's own cigarettes during the war, and who was delighted when my father opened his briefcase and generously gave him a large quantity. Wolfgang loved these journeys, not only because they took him to distant corners of the Norway he had come to love, but most of all, because many of his destinations lay by the sea, and my father always had a passion for the sea.

Wolfgang was an exceptionally handsome man: slim and olive-complexioned, with hair slicked back in the manner of a 1930s film star and an ever-present cigarette hanging from his lips. He had a wonderful sense of humor, a quick wit, and an endearing smile. It was not surprising that he was attractive to women.

Wolfgang Hesse, my father, ca.1940

Shortly after Wolfgang was transferred to Norway by his employer in 1942, he had met Vivi Olaussen in Oslo. She was at that time employed in a local millinery shop. How that encounter came to be, I do not know, but a love affair, which was to have enormous consequences for generations and across the borders of several countries, began very quickly. As the war progressed, Vivi was employed in a factory in Rjukan, her hometown, which lies in the Telemark region in the center of Norway. Since Germany's occupation of Norway in 1940, it had become a region of great struggle between the Norwegian resistance movement and the occupiers. It was also an area of production for "heavy water," a component in the creation of nuclear weapons. My father would later find himself sharing a prison cell in Oslo with a member of the Resistance who had attempted a sabotage raid against a heavy water plant in 1943. When Wolfgang and Vivi were not able to be together due to her work and his travels, they kept in touch by mail. Dozens of these passionate letters written by my father to Vivi are in my possession. Wolfgang was a true romantic and often called her "my beloved Rjukan girl," in reference to the town where she had been born.

In late 1942, my mother Helga followed Wolfgang to Norway, having neither informed nor consulted him. The firm, H. Klammt, must have deemed her services, close to her husband, to be of value. Being an intelligent woman, also facile with languages, she likely was persuasive in convincing her employer that she needed to join her husband and could be of service in Norway herself. My father was less enthused. At her unexpected arrival, and in answer to his question as to what she had done with Gabriele, she simply answered "I gave her to foster parents."

It could not have taken Helga long to learn of the new woman in Wolfgang's life, arousing jealousy, anger, and resentment, for she soon began to spread false rumors about him. She wrote a lie-filled letter to Vivian in order to discredit him and informed Wolfgang's parents in Germany that he was dead. Wolfgang, in turn, described her as a hysterical and sick individual "who made life hell for me." By early 1943, Wolfgang had already initiated divorce proceedings against Helga, which were finalized in Berlin on June 22, 1944, barely three years after their marriage.

On September 20, 1944, Vivi Olaussen gave birth to my half-brother, Rolf Vidar, in Norway. I did not learn of his existence until I was in my forties, and we met for the first time in the summer of 1985, shortly before our father's death.

Helga remained in Norway until February of 1943, creating discord and spreading rumors in whatever way she could. As a result, the company, H. Klammt, sent her back to Germany, no doubt to my father's relief. Helga's presence, with its negative consequences, must have created great consternation for Vivi, until my father informed her by letter that his former wife would no longer be employed by the firm.

While still in Norway, Helga had also found solace with other men, one of whom became the father of a child to whom she gave birth in August 1943, after her return to Germany. That child was my half-sister,

Klaudia, whom I met for the first time in 1988. For over a decade, Helga claimed that this child was Wolfgang's, resulting in a legal battle that did not end until 1955. During all the intervening years, Helga had refused to share the results of her daughter's blood tests, taken annually, which would have proven that Wolfgang was not Klaudia's father. I distinctly remember the evening in Ealing, a borough of London, where we were living by 1955, when my father asked to take a walk with me. He informed me that Helga had at last submitted the required tests, and that the litigation had now been terminated. The final results proved his claims that this child was not his daughter. It made no impact on me at the time, and I remember no reaction on my part. I was thirteen years old and by that time had already lived through so many changes in my life, that the news of the existence of yet another sister left no memorable impression.

For Klaudia, it was traumatic, as I learned when we finally met in 1988. During her early school years, she was known as Klaudia Hesse, based on her mother's claims of Wolfgang's parenthood. At the resolution of the lawsuit, she was one morning called out of the classroom and informed that beginning on that day, she could no longer use the family name of Hesse but would now have to bear our mother's maiden name, Scholze. She was, and is today, still convinced that Wolfgang was her father, all medical proof to the contrary. Helga had also given Klaudia to foster parents, a considerably older Communist couple who had been friends of her parents. Although she was raised in the Eastern and thus Communist part of the divided Germany, I believe her foster parents were as loving as my own.

Chapter 16

Wolfgang Is Arrested

DESPITE THE FACT that war was raging throughout the world, Norway must have appeared a safe haven for my father, following the many disappointments of his life to date. Yet he found no permanent security there either. Rolf was an infant of three months when my now-divorced father attempted to obtain a license in order to marry the woman he loved, Vivi Olaussen. This request alerted the Gestapo to the fact that Wolfgang, contrary to their orders, had been sent out of Germany illegally by his employer. It resulted in his immediate arrest, on December 7, 1944, by the German Security Police (SS), a unit originally established as Hitler's personal bodyguards. Although not informed at the time of the official charges against him or even interrogated, he was accused of having made defeatist statements such as "There is no use in pursuing this war" and having listened to foreign radio broadcasts, accusations that my father denied. There was suspicion that Helga might have had a hand in spreading such rumors as an act of revenge.

It was not until three months after my father's arrest on March 14, 1945, that Vivian Olaussen finally was able to write to the commander of the SS in Oslo to enquire about the whereabouts of her fiancé, Wolfgang Hesse. They replied on March 21, 1945, that they had no knowledge of him. And it was only in November 1945, almost a year after his arrest and imprisonment, and following the end of the war, that

Wolfgang himself was able to write to her for the first time. When her reply finally came, he was overjoyed that she and Rolf were alive. Prior attempts to make contact with her had been rejected by Norwegian, Swedish, and Danish consulates, and the Red Cross had not responded either. It was important to Wolfgang that Vivi and her family should be convinced that he had never been a Nazi, that he had been a strong friend of Norway and its people, a fact for which the Nazis had, in fact, reproached him.

In his joy—and naiveté—Wolfgang implored Vivi and Rolf to come at once to Germany and the small town where he was by then living. "The landscape will remind you a little of southern Norway," he wrote in a euphoric mode; "there was no war damage here at all," as indeed there had not been, except to the souls of its citizens. But it was not to be. Wolfgang and Vivi had no way of knowing at this time that they would never see each other again.

Following his arrest on December 7, 1944, Wolfgang had been immediately transported to a prison in Kristiansand where he was kept in isolation for five days. With the accusations still hanging over him, he was taken by night train to the headquarters of the Nazi Security Police and SS prison at Moellergata, No.19 in Oslo, and put into the so-called German cell, where three German prisoners were already being held. Shortly after Christmas of 1944, my father was moved to the Akershus Fortress, which towers over the bay of Oslo. Here he initially occupied a single cell and later a community cell, and it was probably there that the saboteur of the Rjukan heavy water facility kept him company. Today, this fortress houses the Resistance Museum, which I have since visited in the company of my brother, Rolf.

A court proceeding against Wolfgang was never held in Norway, although he had been threatened with one. Instead, in March 1945, my father, again accompanied by a member of the SS, was taken to the infamous Albrecht Prison in Berlin. This prison was known as the "Home Prison" of the SS and was notorious for the diverse methods of torture applied to individuals in order to obtain desired information. Its inhabitants were mainly political: Communists, socialists, and union members, as well as those belonging to diverse resistance groups. It was not large enough to accommodate more than fifty prisoners, and many were housed elsewhere, only to be brought here for interrogation. Ironically, my father was put up for some time in the administration building of a nearby synagogue, where he shared a cell with a variety of prisoners, "black marketeers, former inmates of concentration camps and young people of doubtful reputation," as he stated in a letter. Women and young girls were kept in an adjoining cell, including foreigners, who were frequently beaten. Russian women were kept in a separate cell, some in cages. According to rumors, Jewish prisoners were kept standing in water in the basement of the building.

Under these circumstances, it was not surprising that my father developed dysentery, diagnosed by two doctors, likewise prisoners, both Jews, one German the other Polish. The diagnosis resulted in his release on March 31, 1945, with instructions not to leave Berlin.

But my father's ordeal was not yet over. Although his former employer, H. Klammt, hired him back at once, he was almost immediately called up by the Volkssturm, a national militia, established on Hitler's orders. It consisted of older and retired soldiers as well as civilians. Their mission was to fight back the approaching Russian army who had launched an attack on the capital on April 16, 1945. It was a useless effort to defend the ruins of Berlin. Eleven days later, on April 27, my father was captured by the Russians in the streets of the city. He was taken to Camp Trebbin, a sub-camp of the better-known concentration camp Sachsenhausen, which the Russians now occupied. While under Nazi control, this had been a brutal camp, with a mission to find the most effective and efficient ways of killing, and it had become a training center for the SS. Their victims were mainly political prisoners, including Joseph Stalin's oldest son, as well as people they wanted dead for religious reasons, such as Jews.

My father spent the following four months in this camp, along with twenty-five thousand other prisoners. In spite of this ordeal, in letters written to his parents, my father stated that the Russians were very decent and fair. He was finally released in September 1945. An unpleasant souvenir of Wolfgang's fighting in defense of Berlin was a bullet discovered lodged in his lung during a routine hospital stay some years later.

Not once did my father actually speak of these experiences in his early life! My parents' generation seemed to be one of silent suffering. They endured, they survived, but then they resumed their lives. I do not recall that "The War" was ever spoken about in my family, nor would I have known what it meant. Our life's circumstances were modest, but having no basis for comparison, I did not know what life had been like before, particularly in families of relative affluence such as mine had been.

Books have been written about this so-called "forgotten generation" to which I belong—a generation that experienced, in more subtle ways, the results of the trauma our parents had been subjected to. No dialogue about the past was ever initiated by my parents, and consequently no curiosity was ever aroused on my part. There was little tenderness or overt affection demonstrated, and I cannot recall that my parents ever actually telling me that they loved me. Perhaps this was, in some measure, also due to the traditional reserve of the German or Prussian character. My role as a child was either to comply or to rebel. For me, it was mostly the latter as I grew older.

Part 2

The War Is Over

Chapter 17

My Father Finds Employment

FOLLOWING HIS TIME as a Russian prisoner of war, Wolfgang returned to the parental home, the apartment over the grocery store in Laasphe, in the western part of Germany. He was penniless and had no clothes; all his personal possessions had been stolen during his several imprisonments. In later years, he was compensated with nominal amounts of money by the German government, not only for his material losses but also for the loss of his freedom due to imprisonment and for the discrimination he suffered as a result of anti-Semitic policies.

Although by birth Wolfgang was only one quarter Jewish, Hitler had extended the definition of Jew to include everyone with even a trace of "Jewish blood." This persecution had affected my half-Jewish grandfather, Walther Hesse, as described earlier, but it had affected his children, and particularly his son, in even greater measure. Many of the decisions concerning compensation did not occur until twelve years or more after the end of the war, and only after many a legal battle, luckily assumed for Wolfgang by his father. It was not until 1957 that the German government officially recognized that my father had been discriminated against on the basis of race, by compensating him with a very small sum of money. Obviously, no amount of money could ever make up for what he did not have in the first place, an education! While my grandfather was again practicing law, Wolfgang still only had his languages, and whatever administration skill he had acquired while employed by H. Klammt, with which to begin a new life.

At the end of World War II, Germany had been divided by the victorious powers into four Allied occupation zones: American, British, French, and Russian. Laasphe in the state of Westphalia, where Wolfgang's parents resided, as well as the nearby small town of Berleburg, now lay in the British Zone. Fortunately, my father almost immediately, in October 1945, found employment as an interpreter, first with the British military government and subsequently, two years later, with the British Control Commission in Berleburg, a mere twelve miles from his parental home.

By land area, Berleburg is considered to be one of the largest towns in Germany. Surrounded by low-lying mountains, it was settled as early as the seventh century, although the town itself never grew to be of significant size. At the time my father lived there, the population was around seven thousand people. Many smaller communities have since been incorporated into what is now a spa town and called "Bath" Berleburg, the spa effects being primarily attributed to the mild climate. A three-winged castle, set within a beautiful park above a series of small lakes, is home to the only black swans I have ever seen. The noble family residing in it at the time was related to the Danish royal house and by extension, to many of the European royal families. Since the sixteenth century, slate has been mined in the region, and many of the exteriors, as well as the roofs, of homes in Laasphe, Berleburg, and the small surrounding communities are covered with this material. It is unique to the area and gives a distinctive if rather dark aspect to the towns.

Among the many documents that I inherited at the time of my father's death was a brief letter of recommendation for Wolfgang, written by Mr. A. H. Ballantyne of the British Legation in Bangkok and dated March 25, 1936. In the letter, this gentleman not only states that my father had "particularly impressed him" while attending his lectures at Heidelberg but also that he had evidenced "marked ability and determination." Though he lacked a university diploma, these were words that stood Wolfgang in good stead many years later and no doubt were helpful in obtaining a position with the British Allies.

During his employment with the British, Wolfgang naturally was able to use his considerable English language skills. His work included interpreting in areas of politics, both at the local as well as the national level; in local administrative matters; in courts of law; and in industry, as well as in all the other spheres of responsibility that now fell under the purview of the local commander of this defeated country.

Although Vivi had been informed that Wolfgang had been arrested and taken out of the country, for almost a year she had no way of knowing where he was or how to be in touch with him. In the years following my father's forced return to Germany, literally hundreds of letters, often written daily, at least on Wolfgang's part, passed between him and his "beloved Vivi." Sometimes the letters crossed or Vivi did not respond in as timely a fashion as my father hoped, and the tone in his next letter became impatient. Apologies then followed, blaming his impatience on his need for her. All my father's letters, at least in the beginning, contained an agonizing sense of longing.

In spite of the fact that World War II had ended in May 1945, travel between Norway and Germany was not permitted by the Allied Powers for at least two years. Both Vivi and Wolfgang attempted to find exemptions to these regulations, on the basis of their having a child, either through contacting the Norwegian Interior Ministry or the Red Cross. They were not successful. Not even the sending of packages for birthdays or Christmas was permitted. Furthermore, following the war's end, both parties were only allowed to correspond in their native language. Early letters to Vivi had been primarily in Norwegian, which Wolfgang now spoke and wrote fluently. Beginning in 1946, however, this changed. Wolfgang was now allowed to write only in German and Vivi to respond only in Norwegian. The letters in my possession are primarily those sent by my father to Vivi in Norwegian as well as some, from later years, when he was obligated to write in German. They had been saved by her, and subsequently by her son, Rolf, in the attic of their home. When I finally met my half-brother, Rolf, in 1985, he generously gave me all the letters my father had sent to his mother, permitting me to keep them.

I had the good fortune of having a cousin who had worked most of her professional life as a translator of several languages for the European

Commission in Luxembourg. She kindly performed the mammoth task of translating these very many Norwegian letters, thus opening an entire chapter of my father's life!

As for letters sent by Vivi to my father, either he destroyed them after his second marriage, or my stepmother did, just as she destroyed all documentation pertaining to my mother's and Wolfgang's divorce, much to my dismay and anger.

Chapter 18

My Father's Life in Berleburg

WOLFGANG OCCUPIED A small furnished apartment in the small town of Berleburg, and having acquired a radio, he was able to reach a frequency that broadcast in Norwegian. He followed their programs in the evenings, as they gave him a sense of connection and allowed him to retain his fluency. Occasionally he was also able to obtain a Norwegian novel through a friend. For the rest of his life, my father subscribed to foreign newspapers, above all Norwegian, but also English, French, and Spanish. Bookshelves in our home always contained a number of foreign language dictionaries.

Since neither Wolfgang nor Vivi was able to travel to the other's country, Wolfgang sought approval for travel to Norway's neighbor, Sweden. In doing so he addressed his request to the Swedish Supervisory Committee in Stockholm in February 1947, with a request for permission to settle in Sweden permanently. This request was denied on the basis that he did not fulfill the prerequisite for settlement, as he had no relatives in that country. On receipt of this denial, in September of that year, Wolfgang wrote to the Interior Ministry of Norway, requesting either an entry permit for himself to Norway or an exit permit for Vivi to leave the country, emphasizing their desire to marry. The letter was returned unopened.

In short, their only hope now rested on the positive conclusion of a pending peace conference and, hopefully, a subsequent peace agreement between Germany and Norway. Wolfgang had written at one point that his dearest wish was to live in Norway "where the people are upright and honest," and he hoped to assume Norwegian citizenship. Emigration to America was another possibility my father had entertained, as he had friends who had promised to help him achieve this and to establish a new existence there. In the event, none of these things came to pass.

As a result of Wolfgang's employment by the British Control Commission, and in addition to doing translations in his free hours, my father was now earning enough money to afford the acquisition of his own furniture and to begin a new life. But hardships still existed, and Wolfgang wrote of these to Vivi. In 1947, the coal shortage in Europe, and particularly in Germany, was enormous, causing a greatly reduced supply of electricity. Often power was interrupted several times a day. Sometimes there was none at all, resulting in cold living quarters. In his parents' rather large apartment in Laasphe, only one room could be heated. Water was in short supply, and only very limited amounts could be drawn from the tap at any one point in the evenings, so that there would be enough for the following morning. Additionally, there was a shortage of food, so my father was grateful for his employment by the British Control Commission who supplied him with extra rations at midday, which they called a "midship meal." The British Commandant and his wife were extraordinarily kind to Wolfgang in other ways, lending him items to facilitate his life in his small apartment, and inviting him, on occasion, to small festivities in their home.

By 1946, Wolfgang had been separated from his "beloved Vivi" for two years. Although that November he wrote to her that he could never have an "honest" relationship with another woman and that he would marry no one if he could not marry her, he had, in fact, already met another woman. He had mentioned this for the first time in April 1946, only a few months after his return to post-war civilian life, by stating rather casually, "I have met someone who impresses me very much." He did not admit until much later that he had become romantically involved or that a child had been born from this union in April 1947. His rationalization for involvement with this woman seemed to be that "unfortunately Gabriele is still with the foster family, will soon be five years old and finally needs a 'good mother.' His concept of a mother for me appears in retrospect to have been a rather interchangeable role, depending on availability.

On a less personal level, my father wrote to Vivi in February 1947 his observation that slowly but surely "we are returning to peaceful conditions. Here, in Germany, it will still take some time, but millions of people seem already to have forgotten that this enormously powerful war-machinery had attacked the entire world and that this world was entitled to defend itself. Unfortunately, much was destroyed in the process, which is entirely the fault of the Nazis. But today they imagine that adversity exists only in Germany and Germany should now become a Paradise. This is nothing but evil propaganda and one has to fight against it with all means" (letter, Wolfgang to Vivi, Feb. 6, 1947).

In spite of his ever more complicated personal situation, Wolfgang continued in his attempts to obtain permission to travel to Norway or to have Vivi come to Germany. He still considered himself to be engaged to her, wearing a wedding band on his left hand that would have been moved to the right on his wedding day, as was customary at the time. He always signed his letters to Vivi as "Your Husband." Wolfgang expressed extreme fear in one of those letters that she, Vivi, might meet another man. He wrote "not because I do not trust you, but because I know that life and circumstances might be stronger than we are and, in any case, three years are a very long time—but only death can part us"!

Throughout 1947, Wolfgang persisted in writing to any agency or person who might be influential in facilitating his return to Scandinavia, whether Norway or Sweden. Among them was Princess Margareta of the Swedish royal house, who was related to a branch of the Berleburg nobility. None of these letters, nor one written to the Swedish Red Cross, ever received a reply. Nor did an appeal to Count Bernadotte, a Swedish diplomat who negotiated the release of thousands of prisoners from German concentration camps, have the desired effect.

By December of that year, in spite of repeated attempts to obtain travel permits for either himself or Vivi, my father seemed to be resigned to the fact that they would not see each other again until a peace agreement had been signed between the two countries at some distant date. Wolfgang expressed extreme "helplessness" and felt that he was "living in a prison." "We have to pay an enormous price for Hitler's criminal government," he wrote just before Christmas 1947.

Beginning in May 1948, a few German nationals were finally permitted to travel to some Scandinavian countries, provided an invitation had been extended by one of their citizens and approved by the local authorities. Norway was not among them.

Dozens of letters continued to be exchanged between Wolfgang and Vivi, the majority written by my father, and often several a week, imploring Vivi to come to Germany. Travel and living arrangements were discussed. Wolfgang required Vivi's commitment to marry him or he would not be able to apply for an apartment to accommodate the "family." He had limited funds and needed to know what she could contribute by way of bringing household goods and bedding.

To no avail! Vivi, apparently convinced by her parents that postwar conditions in Germany were far worse than in Norway and, furthermore, that Wolfgang was not to be trusted, now believed that their marriage might result in a "fiasco." She expressed doubt that she still loved Wolfgang as much as she had previously. Strangely, she resented the fact that their son, Rolf, looked so much like his father.

Although Vivi was by this time aware of Wolfgang's liaison, which had again resulted in a child, Wolfgang made one last attempt, in July 1949, to convince her to come to Germany, sending her a telegram with the following words: "Wire exact arrival until 19 July inclusive or I go away." Vivi not only never came, but instead began to write letters accusing Wolfgang of a "crime" and suggesting that he should be "castrated." He believed that she had now come to hate him.

Chapter 19

Wolfgang Takes Control of His Life

ALTHOUGH IN AUGUST 1949 Wolfgang had briefly contemplated committing suicide, he was also aware that he needed to put his chaotic personal life in order without going to these extremes. In view of Vivi's refusal to come to Germany, in September 1949 he finally married the woman—Miss Reuter or "the girl," as he had often referred to her in his letters—with whom he now had a third child. He had frequently emphasized to Vivi that he wished to have a "mother" for his child from his first marriage to Helga, and he had wanted Vivi to be that "mother." Now the "girl" had to assume that responsibility.

Wolfgang never forgot Vivi and continued to correspond with her for decades, although the declarations of love ceased. In one of these letters, following his new marriage, he mentions that he and Vivi had so perfectly understood each other on every level that he knew he had lost something "that in its completeness" he would never find again—and that he wished he had been more aware of this on September 26, 1949, his wedding day with Miss Reuter.

Wolfgang, now the father of three children, none of whom lived with him, had to make some choices as to their well-being. Most urgently he was concerned with me, his first-born, Gabriele, his daughter by his brief and unfortunate marriage to Helga Scholze. The urgency was exacerbated by the fact that in 1948 I was still living with the one surviving foster parent, my "mother," in what had now become the Russian Zone of this newly divided Germany. The borders between the two zones were quickly closing. While the Russians had been allies of the Americans and British in defeating the evils of National Socialism in Germany, they were now inflicting another form of totalitarianism, namely Communism, on the neighboring countries of Europe. It was Winston Churchill who had stated in a speech during a tour of America in 1946 that "an Iron Curtain has descended across the continent." And in 1948 I was still living behind that "Iron Curtain."

Chapter 20

Gabriele, the Firstborn

AS A RESULT of my father's serial love affairs, in 1948 I was the firstborn of his three children, and the only product of a marriage. My birth took place in Berlin-Schoeneberg on October 19, 1941, one day before my father's own birthday, October 20. It was hardly an auspicious year to be born. I was the result of a confusing mix of social differences, religions, and cultures and entered a world of conflict and turmoil, conditions that were to be mirrored in my own life.

Early photographs show my birth mother as a very young woman of short stature, slim, with wide hips and a mop of red curly hair. The poses are usually alluring; a few exist with me as an infant in her arms. In reality, I know her only through these photos.

At the time of their marriage, Wolfgang and Helga occupied an apartment on a pretty, tree-lined street in the section of Berlin called Schoeneberg. An independent village when first mentioned in historical records in AD 1264, it was not incorporated into the city of Berlin until 1920. Much of it was destroyed by Allied bombing during World War II, as indeed was somewhere between a third and a half of all housing in Germany. In the last days of April 1945, this section of Berlin was occupied by the Russians, although later, upon partitioning of the city, Schoeneberg became part of the American sector. By then I was living elsewhere with my foster parents.

One of Berlin's most significant symbols since the completion of its construction in 1869 is the Red City Hall in Schoeneberg. It is the seat of the mayor as well as the Berlin senate, and it was here that the American President John F. Kennedy, made his speech in June 1963 in which he stated in incorrect German, *"Ich bin ein Berliner"* ("I am a Berliner"), thereby announcing to its citizens that he was a donut, *ein Berliner* being the local expression for that sweet pastry. Of course, his intent was to proclaim his sense of identity with the people of Berlin, and that is how the statement was received. In addition to holding my birth records, this city hall had also played a significant role in the life of my maternal grandfather, whose life I would only learn about at a much later date.

Chapter 21

Helga Gives Me Away

AN APARTMENT ON the Berchtesgadener Strasse, No. 25, in Berlin-Schoeneberg became the first address of my life. Today, several of the houses in the district and of that era are considered cultural monuments. Schoeneberg itself was home to many notable people in the nineteenth and twentieth centuries, particularly those involved in the arts, among them, the actress Marlene Dietrich and the film director Billy Wilder.

I lived there with my parents until August 1942, when my father was sent to Norway. Shortly after his departure, my mother deposited me with a friend of her mother's, whom I never knew on any conscious level. By October 1942, when Helga decided to follow Wolfgang to Norway, I had been given into the care of a married couple, Martha and Arthur Pohl. Both had come from modest backgrounds. At the time they assumed responsibility for me, they were already in their forties having been born in 1898 and 1897, respectively, and were themselves parents of a grown daughter, a nurse named Ursula. Martha had been employed in my grandmother Scholze's household in Berlin, while Arthur worked for the German railway system. They agreed to take me in as a foster child, a fact of which my father was only made aware after Helga's arrival in Norway. When asked by my helpless father what she had done with his daughter, she simply announced that she had given me away.

Early in the war, Arthur Pohl had been inducted into the Army as a low-level soldier but was soon released, as he had contracted tuberculosis. His wife, Martha, was a sturdy, matronly woman of enormous warmth. Only one photo has survived from those years of the three of us as a family. We are enjoying a picnic in the woods, Arthur in uniform. They were the "parents" of my early years. After my foster father's death in the spring of 1948, I remained with Martha alone until I was almost seven years old. She loved me as if I were her own child, and their daughter Ursula, after her marriage, named her own daughter Gabriele. My good fortune was that I had been left in the care of a warm and caring family with whose descendants I am still connected. I have never missed my birth mother.

It was decades before I gave much thought to the turbulence of my life, and only after much reflection did I come to the realization that I had been born at the crossroads of history, into a family of divergent cultures and political beliefs. How we live our lives is dictated not only by our genetics but to a large degree by the events occurring around us as we mature, which are not of our making. War was devastating the world, but my childhood memories are happy ones. Perhaps it was a childhood better than that of many another child, for the simple reason that from the earliest it was filled not only with love but also with change, with a diversity of experiences that some would consider harmful to a child's well-being. While these changes were obviously imposed upon me, and not of my choosing, they certainly helped me adapt in a nonconstant world and seem to have done no harm.

Chapter 22

My Life with Foster Parents—and Beyond

THE FOSTER MOTHER who raised me until age seven was 'de facto' my mother. While Helga apparently made an occasional appearance in my early life, I have no memory of her, had no inkling of who she was, and was far too young to understand that she had given birth to me. The love and nurturing I experienced came from Martha Pohl, the woman into whose care I had been given several months after my birth.

Initially, both families, my birth mother's and my future foster parents, lived in Berlin. When the bombing of Berlin by the Allies accelerated, and there were nightly alarms, my new family and I moved to the small town of Genthin, about eighty miles west of the city. Although I have no active memories of being in bomb shelters in Berlin, there are "flickerings" in my subconscious of being confined, of huddling under low ceilings, and of clutching a small teddy bear—but, above all, of the deafening noise of thousands of airplanes. To this day the sound of an airplane's engine still frightens me.

A photo of myself aged one and a half years is inscribed on the back with the date 1943, and the words that it was taken "just before we were bombed in Berlin." Hitler had, in fact ordered in 1940, and so before my birth, that children should be sent to the countryside, and away from targeted cities. Older children were accompanied by teachers or youth leaders and accommodated in youth hostels, hotels or school buildings. For the Pohl family, to whom I now 'belonged,' our new home would be an apartment in Genthin, and it is to this address that I trace my earliest memories.

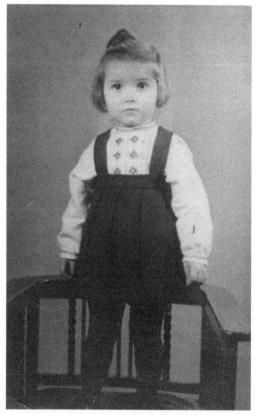

Gabriele at 1 ½ years old in Berlin, just before the bombing

Genthin is situated less than twenty miles from the city of Brandenburg, where much of the lives of my paternal great-grandparents, my grandparents, and even my father had played out. Historically, Genthin was not a town of great significance. Dates vary as to when it was first mentioned in documents, but AD 1171 seems to be generally accepted. Several times over the centuries it almost burned to the ground, and in 1682–83 it was struck by a plague, which killed much of the population.

The Protestant Church of St. Trinity is considered to be its architectural highlight. Built on the site of a former Romanesque church, which was torn down due to structural deficiencies, it was replaced by a Baroque church during the years 1707–1722. However, funds were lacking to complete a bell tower. Although the Prussian King Frederick I admired this new construction and thought it beautiful enough even for the capital city, Berlin, when asked for monies to complete the tower, he responded that such a "dump" of a town should build its own tower for a hundred Taler (dollars), the equivalent value of which in today's currency I cannot begin to guess. In short, he was not inclined to contribute. His son, Frederick the Great, known as "Old Fritz," showed himself more generous in later years and agreed to pay for the completion of the tower out of State funds. The 50-meter bell tower was thus completed by 1772.

Many streets in Genthin are laid out so that they lead, like sunbeams, directly to St. Trinity, and it was down one of these streets I was led on March 10, 1946, by my foster parents in order to be christened. I was almost four and a half years old, unusually old for such an event, but I learned in later years that Helga had not wished for me to be christened at all. Coming as she did from a Communist and nonreligious background, she perhaps did not want to inflict a religious belief system on her child, if she thought about me as her child at all. Assumedly my father, born of Jewish forebears but raised as a Protestant himself, prevailed, perhaps in order to affirm my own Protestant and Prussian heritage. Whatever the reasoning, the ceremony took place, and I distinctly recall wiping the drops of "holy water" from my forehead. I stood again beside the same baptismal font in the summer of 2018, this time as a tourist, in front of a camera and accompanied by my husband.

In addition to the christening, there are two clear memories that remain with me from a time when I could not have been more than four years old. The most significant one speaks of war and the fact that people were hungry. Our apartment in Genthin was located on an upper floor of a nondescript building with a view of the street. It was always referred to as the "chaussée," the French term for a paved road, and it was here where I usually played, either spinning tops or playing ball with other children. Looking out of the window one day, I witnessed a dead horse, a rope slung around its neck, being dragged along this road, followed by a desperately running crowd of people. At that young age, of course I could not realize that they were driven by hunger and, in retrospect, can only guess at the ravaging of this poor animal. To this day, it is a scene I have never forgotten and can still visualize.

A second memory, also very distinct, and perhaps indicative of what was even then an impatient personality, pertains to my own head of hair. Fashion for little girls at the time dictated that the hair be wound around a small comb and pinned to the top of the head. Many photographs of those years show young girls sporting such a 'coiffure.' It was during my mother's absence one day when frustration arose in my inability to remove this comb. The logical step seemed to be to reach for a pair of scissors and cut off both, comb and hair. My mother was not amused, but I do not recall the ensuing punishment.

Following a period of convalescence after his diagnosis of tuberculosis, my foster father, Arthur Pohl, resumed work for the railroad system and in that capacity was assigned responsibility for a very small railroad station in the village of Ferchland. This tiny community, just north of the county seat of Genthin, lies directly on the banks of one of Europe's great rivers, the Elbe, which originates in the Czech Republic, passes through some of the world's most important cities such as Dresden and Hamburg, and eventually flows into the North Sea. The entire area is known as the Mark Brandenburg.

Not only was the Mark Brandenburg the region where my paternal grandfather had lived in Gransee, and where his children were born, but it was also the beloved terrain of one of Germany's favorite writers, Theodor Fontane. Born in 1819 near Berlin, a pharmacist by training, he was later a journalist and became what is considered to be Germany's most important representative of "literary realism." Two of his novels, such as *Effi Briest* and *Grete Minde*, are both based on true events, both have tragic endings, and both were made into films in the 1970s. In addition, Fontane wrote what is probably his best-known work, the five-volume series called *Wanderings through Mark Brandenburg*, a travelogue of the times, in which he describes the physical attributes and the beauty of the landscape surrounding Berlin. It is here, in Germany's capital, that he died in 1898.

Ferchland, which lies in this region, was probably occupied as early as the Stone Age, although officially it is not mentioned in documents until AD 1302. It never grew into a significant community, having only about eight hundred inhabitants at the beginning of the twentieth century. Nevertheless, it became an important part of my childhood memories and has drawn me back more than once. It was here that my small toes first touched the shallow waters on the banks of the Elbe River into which I waded on summer days. Only a ferry was available for the crossing of the river at this point, but it was exactly here, on April 29, 1945, that a prisoner exchange took place between the 9th US Army and the German troops, led by General Wenck, who had been fighting in the region. A week later, on May 7, 1945, at 5:00 p.m. this same general, together with his chief of staff, boarded the last boat to cross the Elbe River in order to become prisoners of war of the Americans. All this history played out within little more than one mile of where I was living with my foster parents in the railroad station.

The train station itself, an insignificant building that still stands today on the perimeter of the village, was also where the stationmaster and his family lived. It was to be the new home of Arthur and Martha Pohl and their foster child, Gabriele. The station was a two-story affair in which I vaguely remember a ticket counter and a waiting area downstairs, while we resided on the upper floor. The train tracks were located in front of the station building, while the back abutted a dense forest of the typical German coniferous kind. It was a wonderful place for a child to explore, to gather berries and to make a serious project of collecting mushrooms (although not always of the edible kind).

The station was somewhat isolated from the village, and I was forced to find my own amusements, as there were no other children close by. At some point I was enrolled in the kindergarten of the village, which I happily attended, with a little brown leather bag, worn across my body, containing whatever was available for a snack. But my greatest joy was to ride the electric train. It connected a number of small communities, passing our station several times daily. Once each day I was allowed to board it and travel the two stops to the end of the line, where the last passengers would be discharged. I would then be brought back to "my own" station. Reflecting on this memorable ritual, I can only imagine the smiles of the train personnel as I boarded and settled into my seat, always with a little shoulder bag that contained folded bits of paper, a pencil and most importantly, a nail file. At the time, I could neither read nor write, but clean fingernails were a 'must.' Even today the contents of my handbag must contain these same items. I have no doubt that this short daily voyage and the idea of movement, of going to a place distant from home, sowed the seeds for my love of travel, which has never left me.

Ferchland Train Station

Ours was a simple life in every sense of the word. There were few material goods. I have no remembrance of toys, although, at the end of the war, no doubt thanks to American care packages, I was fortunate to have received a doll and even a small dollhouse. On occasion, notably at Christmastime, there would be a package from my maternal grandmother, Martha Scholze, who resided in Berlin but whom, to my knowledge, I had never met. She would send what she could, such as chocolate, coffee, and biscuits. These things never seemed to arrive in time for the holiday, and letters between my foster mother and the "unknown" grandmother speak of tracing such packages because "Gaby was very disappointed" that nothing had arrived. Obviously, there was much disruption in institutions such as the postal service following the war.

I took great pride and found much happiness in the little garden I had created on the far side of the railroad tracks. Not only did I grow flowers, but with great anticipation, I watched the ripening progress of my strawberries from green to pale red on a daily basis. These strawberries were also the reason for one of the great tragedies of my young life, as one morning I found that the berries, in their still unripe state, were gone! I was devastated. Somehow, I seemed to know who had stolen them and persuaded my mother that we needed to pay a visit to the probable culprit's home and demand their return. It was the father of the "accused," a little kindergarten friend of mine, who received us. My accusations must have sounded credible, as I received an orange in exchange for the berries, which were by then probably long devoured. I had never seen an orange before and have no recollection as to what my reaction was. But to receive such an exotic fruit during these years of deprivation, and such a short time after the end of the war, must have been wonderful for my mother. Perhaps I was persuaded that justice had been done.

There is a later chapter to this little anecdote. In July 1990, just a few months after the wall dividing the two Germanys had fallen, I was able to realize the dream of returning to the place of my happy early years. My husband had long been familiar with my childhood stories and was equally interested to see where I had lived. It was with some trepidation that we approached the border by car from the West to the now dismantling East. We did not have the documents that the newspapers claimed were required to make this crossing, and I was extremely nervous. But the East German military guards, who in the past would have searched every inch of every vehicle attempting to cross this border, now could not wave the masses through fast enough. The relief of suddenly reaching the other side of this earlier impediment, unharmed and not confronted with rifles, caused me to burst into tears.

It was a quite different Germany we now had entered. The word *colorless* is perhaps the best descriptor. It was as if the clock had been turned back, as if it were still 1948. The houses were old, none had seen repair or paint in many a decade. Maintaining property in good condition had long been impossible in the East due to the lack of materials. The streets were in poor condition, many still cobblestoned, just as I remembered them from my childhood. Local residents peeked out from behind white lace curtains to observe the streams of western cars passing by. Time had stood still here.

When I had left this tiny village forty-two years before, it was with fear and in tears. My return to it was a moment of joy. It is impossible to describe the excitement I felt as the first to greet us was the two-car electric train rolling across the horizon as we entered Ferchland. I grabbed my husband by the sleeve. "Look, look, that is my train!" I shouted. Had we been expected? Had someone ordered it to welcome me back forty-two years later? Could it really be by chance that on this particular day, at this particular moment, one of my most vivid childhood memories was brought back to life?

Throughout the decades following my departure, I had lost touch with my foster family. Although I had been too young to keep up correspondence, my parents must have informed me at some point that my foster mother was no longer alive. But I remembered that she had a daughter whom she had named after me. What had become of her? Perhaps there were other family members to be found.

Knowing only the last name of my foster mother's descendants, we stopped in the tiny town hall of the village to enquire about them. Such questions were greeted with great suspicion. Hardly had the two Germanys been reunited when scavengers of property began arriving from the West to lay claim to lands or buildings that had long ago passed to new owners during the Communist era. We were assumed to be among such scavengers.

Following my explanation of why we were there, convincing the town hall staff that our only mission was to find relatives of my foster family, we were finally given an address to which we directly drove. We arrived at the same instant as a pleasant-looking woman of early middle age exited her car. I introduced myself, and she was flabbergasted, explaining that just the night before the family had spoken of me, wondering what had become of me. Could life really be filled with so many coincidental events? Forty-two years after my departure I had been thought about and spoken of, and the following day I arrived!

We were very warmly received by two and even three later generations of my foster family. It was truly as if they had been expecting us. Indeed, they told us that the evening before my arrival they had looked at photographs of me with my "parents," the Pohls. Coffee and cake were immediately produced, and a wizened old lady of my foster mother's generation, and somehow related to this family, told me that she recognized my smile. None, however, were able to answer any of the questions pertaining to my childhood or knew the location of the kindergarten I had attended here so many years before. It was suggested I should meet with the mayor of the village, on the assumption that he might have records. An appointment was made for that very same evening at 6:00 p.m. and the meeting place was to be the village hall. Naturally, the mayor had been told whom to expect and why I was there.

At the appointed hour, a man of approximately my own age was waiting for me. While exchanging pleasantries, he claimed that his wife, who would shortly join us, knew me. This I found hard to fathom, as I had not been in Ferchland in more than forty-two years, nor had I been in contact with anyone during those many decades. I was no wiser when his wife arrived a few minutes later. She identified herself with only her first name, but I remained mystified. It brought back no memories. Finally, I asked the pertinent question: "Were you by any chance the little girl who stole my strawberries?" She confessed, with lowered eyes, and even then, so many years later, the body language of shame. She recounted that as a result of her theft, she had received a severe whipping from her father.

In 2018, when I again visited this part of Germany, my destination was the town of Genthin, where I had lived during the bombing of Berlin and where I had been christened. Here I wished to locate the address of the *chaussée* and house number where I had lived with my foster parents. I made my way to the rather grand red brick building of the old town hall, its architecture being very typical for this part of Germany in the 1890s. The building was practically vacant as it was lunchtime, a sacred hour in the German workday. Eventually I located an office shared by two women who seemed to be the sole employees not having left the building to take advantage of this free time. To them I explained my hope of finding the significant address of my early childhood.

A pleasant conversation soon established that one of the women herself lived in Ferchland, less than ten miles distant, and that she was in fact the daughter of the strawberry thief. She had not been familiar with her mother's 'criminal background,' and it goes without saying that we shared a good deal of laughter. Obviously, fate had decided that instead of going to lunch, she should await my arrival. The address I had hoped to find could not be located, but this humorous exchange was fine compensation.

In spite of the happy memories I cherished, I know that the years I had spent here had been extraordinarily difficult times for a country once again defeated in war. While I do not recall ever being hungry, that was probably due to sacrifices made by my foster parents. I do have a very clear recollection of walking across the stubble of harvested wheat fields in bare feet to see what might have been left behind, as well as searching for potentially overlooked potatoes in the ground.

The first great sadness and personal loss I consciously experienced in my young life occurred in April 1948, when my foster father died of tuberculosis. I can almost still hear the church bells ringing, calling the mourners to his funeral, and I have a vivid memory of myself, sitting and crying on the steps of the little train station, dressed in a dark green coat. In fact, 1948 was to become a year of totally unanticipated sorrow and upheaval for me, in ways that far exceeded the death of my foster father.

Chapter 23

I Am Taken Away

AFTER GERMANY'S CAPITULATION ended the war, the country was divided into the previously mentioned four sectors. Each was administered by one of the victorious Allied powers, one of which was Russia. These powers were intended to restore order and return life to some sort of normalcy.

With my foster parents, I now lived in the eastern part of this demolished land, an area primarily occupied by the Russians and, according to Winston Churchill, geographically located behind the descending Iron Curtain. My father, who was still working for the British Control Commission, was in the West. In his letters to Vivi, Wolfgang had spoken of the fact that there were again rumblings of war in 1948. The remaining Allies, consisting of the United States, Great Britain, and France, contemplated uniting their sectors of Berlin into one. Russia viewed this as a threat and retaliated with a blockade. Berlin itself was isolated, and only very limited travel to and from the Eastern Zone was permitted.

As a result of Helga's false accusation that Wolfgang had been a Nazi Party member—ridiculous on its face, as he had been persecuted and imprisoned by them, due to his Jewish heritage—Wolfgang had voiced his protests to the legal authorities. He was subsequently declared to be my sole guardian and now had to find a way to get me out of the Russian Zone as quickly as possible. The end of October 1948 was the deadline for such permitted departures. In June of that year, he reiterated to Vivi that it was *she* whom he wished to marry and that *she* was to become my "mother"—indeed, that he would never marry anyone else! It seems he believed that being a mother could be a delegated and interchangeable function. "Gabriele on the other hand, apparently bursts into tears every time mention is made of having to leave her foster mother," Wolfgang wrote to Vivi. Of course, I had no choice in the matter.

On a very dark October night in 1948, I was taken away, never to see my foster mother again. I stood for the last time on our little station platform, tearful and frightened, a small suitcase at my side, accompanied by a man who may have been a family friend but of whom I have no distinct memory. He was to accompany me to the city of Helmstedt, about sixty miles away, which constituted the border between Russian-occupied East Germany and the West. From here trains departed several times daily for cities in the Western zone. Whether we were headed to one of the frequent destinations of Berlin or Cologne, I do not know.

At the train station I was handed over to a woman I had never seen before, who had agreed to bring me to the West. I later learned that she was the sister of my grandfather Hesse's secretary in his newly reestablished law practice. She had been visiting relatives in the Eastern zone and was returning to her home near Laasphe. Since the Russians were unwilling to issue passes to anyone wishing to permanently leave the Eastern zone, I assume that I was smuggled out by the returning woman, who must have represented me as her child.

We were on one of the last trains allowed out by the Russians. Our ultimate destination was to be the home of my paternal grandparents, whom of course I did not know either. It is possible to view a brief video on our electronic devices today that documents one of these last trains leaving the station of Helmstedt in October 1948. It has recorded the many desperately running people who were scrambling to obtain space on the train in order to escape the Communist regime that had now been imposed on that part of the country.

When I allow myself to relive these scenes, my eyes often still well up with tears these many decades later. It was a dramatic and traumatic event for a child. I had left the only mother I had ever known or would ever know. Above all, I did not understand *why* I had to leave, *what* I might have done wrong, or *why* I was being punished. The people who now controlled me were perfect strangers, and I had no idea who these grandparents were to whom I was being taken. It was the month of my seventh birthday.

How long or complicated the journey to my grandparents' home in Laasphe was I cannot recall. Although the war was over, the country was still in a state of upheaval, and trains were not reliable. Certainly, they were not comfortable. My only memory is of wooden benches. Even today, such a train journey takes many hours. Undoubtedly, I was tired and tearful when I was delivered into the kitchen of my grandparents' apartment, where my grandmother Kaethe was grinding coffee beans.

My memory easily takes me back to that moment. I can relive my first view of her and know exactly where she stood, this slim and elegant woman with dark hair, dressed in blue, who turned toward me as I came through the door. The smell of coffee was pervasive; I sense it still— remembrance of things past! The wooden coffee mill has remained in the family and is treasured by my translator cousin, who inherited it.

Chapter 24

A New Home for Gabriele

I ENTERED MY grandparents' apartment fearful and confused. Everybody and everything was unfamiliar. Who were they? The word *grandparents* meant nothing to me, as I had never had any! This was now to be my home? I had never even encountered my father on any conscious level and most certainly had never met or even knew of the existence of these people, his parents, to whom I had now been entrusted.

I was later told that I had been dressed like a child of extreme poverty, that I looked like an orphan. Most likely I would not have been too clean, having just survived an endless journey on a steam train, not in the least like the little electric train I had so much loved in Ferchland. When I finally met the "strawberry thief" many years later, she told me that her father had been the shoemaker of the town, and it was he who had constructed my "travel shoes" from an old leather briefcase, with soles made of wood.

In time, I grew to love my grandmother, who was warm and welcoming. My grandfather seemed rather more forbidding, rotund, bald, and more or less absent from any involvement with me other than admonishing bad behavior.

The apartment over the grocery store, where my grandparents resided, appeared enormous to me, which it certainly was compared to my beloved train station. A large kitchen, containing a stove fed with coal, overlooked the garden belonging to the owners of the building. The kitchen fronted on a long, dark corridor that ended in a bathroom with a bathtub. I had never before seen a bathtub, and in fact, its usage here was restricted to once a week, when Elvira, the maid who came in daily, would give me a bath. There was a shortage of water as well as coal during these cold winter months, and rather than bathe daily, I would have to stand in the middle of the kitchen in the evening, with a bowl of water placed on a stool, so that I could wash my little body. Even at that tender age, this activity embarrassed me.

On either side of the long corridor, there were several bedrooms, as well as a formal dining room. The bedroom immediately adjacent to the kitchen had been assigned to my great-grandmother, Kaethe's mother: Marie von Wilm Schrader, widow of Professor Dr. Otto Schrader. At over ninety years of age, she was confined to her bed, close to death, and it was a frightening sight for a child.

It was Marie and her daughter Else who had been warned by her son, General Rudolf Schrader, my grandmother's brother, to escape from Breslau and make their way to the West during the last days of the war. They were now living as refugees with my grandparents, much to my grandfather's displeasure. Although it was not to his liking, it had in fact been decreed by the government that residents of the West were obligated to accommodate refugees from those parts of Germany that were now occupied by the Russians. My grandparents' bedroom was adjacent to the bathroom at the far end of the long corridor. A lady's dressing table of blond wood with a mirror occupied one wall. I remember that my grandmother's nightstand always contained a bowl of dried figs, an unfamiliar delicacy.

My favorite room in the apartment, however, was the so-called "gentlemen's room." It accommodated heavy leather furniture, a large desk, and an enormous bookcase with a glass front, which held my grandfather's books, some of them huge volumes with pictures of plants and animals. They greatly interested me, as I had never been exposed to books of that kind or size, but they were far heavier than I could hold. Additionally, there was a chaise lounge on which my grandmother took her afternoon rest and, most impressive of all, a radio that I had never before encountered either. How strange to hear voices and music coming out of that box! This was the room to which my grandfather withdrew to read the newspapers and to smoke his endless cigars.

A new era now began for me. Previously I had lived the life of an only child with few constraints. Suddenly I had to behave and abide by rules. There was a gong in the hallway, and when it sounded, I had to present myself at table for a meal. Having appeared, I had to display clean fingernails, and never was I permitted to sit at the table without wearing my shoes.

My grandmother Katharina Hesse in midlife

Until I began my new life in the grandparental home, I had been exposed to little education and had been left very much to my own devices during the years with my foster parents. Although I had briefly attended kindergarten while still living in Ferchland, on arriving in Laasphe, I spoke grammatically incorrect German, and I barely knew how to read at age seven. My grandparents were in their sixties, and it must have been a burden to them to suddenly again have a lively child living under their roof.

Not long after I became a member of their household, the "unwanted" great-aunt, my grandmother's sister Else, had to vacate her bedroom so that it could accommodate their newest refugee, myself. Else moved into a small apartment of her own within walking distance of my grandparents. She had been a schoolteacher in Breslau in the East prior to her escape from the Russian advances, and she now had a new pupil in me. Although I was quickly enrolled in elementary school upon my arrival in my new home, my shortcomings were soon apparent, and I was required to visit this great-aunt every day after classes so she might teach me how to read. I did so with trepidation. She was "old" and to my mind, unattractive and forbidding, wearing the earlier mentioned patch over the eye that she had lost as a result of her tennis accident. In exchange for her teaching, and her patience, I had to thread her sewing needles that she found difficult to do with only one functioning eye.

To this day, I am aware that I owe her immense gratitude, for she awoke in me a tremendous passion for reading. While my grandfather's book collection was certainly too advanced for me, we were fortunate in that tenants living in the apartment above my grandparents, allowed me free access to their attic, where they had stored boxes of their own, now grown children's books. And once I had achieved a reading level commensurate with my age, I devoured them.

It seems that I quickly adjusted to life with my grandparents in Laasphe. My father's sister Gerda, her husband Martin, and their three children lived very close by, and I suddenly had a playmate of my own age in my cousin Monika. We had been born one month apart in 1941. I was the dark-haired child with short hair, she the blond one with long golden braids, which I always envied. We became good company for each other and remain so to this day. The family lived on the same street as my grandparents, on the lower floor of a house near the railway station. In their home I experienced real family life, a father and mother with three children, for the first time.

The war had not yet been over very long, and after such immense destruction, many of life's necessities continued to be in short supply.

Toilet paper in their house consisted of torn pieces of newspaper attached to a nail in the wall. Food was scarce and rationed, yet my aunt always managed to assemble a meal and even create a birthday party. I was treated to a green gelatin dessert called "Wobbly Peter" for the first time. The family included me in their outings, simple pleasures such as walks in the wonderful woods surrounding Laasphe, picking berries or merely gathering wildflowers in a field. I became the fourth member of the grandchildren who had to memorize poems, always composed by my aunt, and reciting them for the grandparents on special occasions such as birthdays or Christmas Eve. And Uncle Martin did not forget me either when he built doll cradles for his young daughters at Christmas time. Gerda would always remain my favorite aunt and, in a sense, a substitute mother for some time.

As I became accustomed to my new environment, my grandparents assigned minor responsibilities to me. A small town, such as they lived in, had specialty shops in addition to the grocery store over which their apartment was located. A nearby bakery delivered fresh warm rolls to the apartment door every morning, but milk had to be purchased in a milk shop in the desired quantities. I was often sent to fetch it in a one-liter aluminum can with lid and handle, especially meant for this purpose. Sometimes I would be permitted to return my grandfather's empty wine bottles for a refund of a few pennies to the grocery store below, which in turn I was allowed to exchange for small quantities of sweets. My grandparents also instilled in me a sense of honesty. When one day I arrived home with an apple in hand, I was asked where I had obtained it. I had to admit that I had reached through the fence of a neighbor's garden and helped myself to it, as it had fallen to the ground. After a scolding, I dutifully returned it to where I had found it.

Winter came soon after my arrival in this new environment, and with it pleasures I had never before experienced. For the first time in my life, I went tobogganing on the hills surrounding the town, together with my cousin and school friends. Where I had lived before, the terrain was much too flat for such pastimes. In the summer, the local swimming pool was our destination. We pleaded to be allowed to go as soon as the water had reached a still very chilly eighteen degrees Centigrade. At that time, I did not know how to swim, but the enjoyment was being with other children, so rare compared to all the previous years of my life.

While my earliest years hold dear the memory of my little railroad station in Ferchland, my attachment to Laasphe is an even stronger one. I need only close my eyes to visualize the town. Like most German communities, and particularly those built centuries ago, at their heart lies the church, around which the residential and commercial structures later developed. I have mentioned that the town was primarily a Lutheran and extremely pious community. When the church is mentioned, it is understood that it means the simple white structure and steeple of the Protestant Church. At its construction in the thirteenth century, it was not given a name, and as the Reformation was introduced into the area in the middle of the sixteenth century, none was needed, as primarily Lutherans resided here. The church was simply *their* church. A Catholic church of much more contemporary architecture was added centuries later as the town grew.

It is assumed that the name *Laasphe* is derived from the old Celtic word *lassaffa*, meaning "salmon water." As the town lies on the River Lahn, a tributary of the Rhine, it was perhaps in prior years the source of this fish. The previously described widespread use of slate in the region is particularly true of Laasphe. The exteriors and roofs of many houses are today still covered with this material. The main thoroughfare, called King Street, was still cobblestoned, and an old fountain, dating to 1667, graced its center when I arrived there.

Many of the side streets are even now lined with beautifully preserved historic, beamed houses, most dating to the seventeenth and eighteenth centuries. They are still occupied. The date of their construction and the names of the original owners are usually painted or carved over the doorways. It is a photographer's paradise. While I only occasionally accompanied my grandmother to a church service, the sentimental memory remained with me throughout the years, so that when I planned to be married for the second time in 1984, it was in the Protestant church of Laasphe where I wanted the religious ceremony of my marriage to Sylvester Miniter to take place.

The church in Laasphe

In January of 1949, not long after my arrival from the East, my grandmother wrote to Vivi, whom my father was still hoping and planning to marry during that year, "While Gabriele is a dear, lovable and happy child, always willing to help, she is also quite wild and needs to be reined in. You will not have any problems with her." My grandmother was expecting and accepting Vivi Olaussen to be her new daughter-in-law and my new mother. She hoped that the children, Rolf and Gabriele, would get along well together, but she also emphasized that Gabriele had not yet been told that she would have a "new mother." At the time, only three months after my arrival in the grandparental home, I was still in mourning for the mother I had lost, and my grandmother felt that there was plenty of time to prepare me for a new one. When my grandmother wrote "wild," she meant lively, in that I was always an active child, always talking. It reflected in my schoolwork and behavior. It was, therefore, a great surprise to me when many decades later I received an invitation from a first-year classmate in Laasphe to attend a class reunion of the elementary school. My first thought was that his memory of me must have been of my back, as I was often made to stand in the corner due to excessive chattering.

Chapter 25

Who Will Be My New Mother?

IN JUNE 1949, Wolfgang reminded Vivi that they had both agreed on the month of July for her arrival in Germany. He stated that it had to be specifically between the fourth and the twenty-sixth, as he would only be able to take vacation during that time from his job at the British Control Commission. My father wished to welcome and spend time with her. His own work was extremely time-consuming, but he wanted to help her adjust to her new environment.

Wolfgang again pressed for her commitment to become his wife, which she seemed reluctant to give, although he firmly stated that she had a "first right" to him. Such language must have set off alarm bells in Vivi. If she had the first right, then she might have asked herself who was next in line? Wolfgang wanted her as his wife and as a mother for Gabriele. But his letters had become less personal, less passionate, and more practical by this time. He recognized and wrote to her that during these many years of fighting for permanence in their relationship, they both, no doubt, had changed.

Finally, Wolfgang informed Vivi that he had begun another relationship, and that this "girl" had a child. Almost as an unimportant aside, in one sentence of this letter he explained that this "girl," who had lost her father and brother during the war, had also lost her home to bombs and all her money due to currency reform but that "she had never pressed him to marry her". It was no doubt this last sentence that finally told the whole story, that the child belonging to this "girl" was Wolfgang's. Seven years had elapsed since the beginning of Wolfgang's and Vivi's romance, and five years had passed since they had last seen each other—years filled with hundreds of letters, emotions expressed only on paper, hopes elevated and dashed, and a final acceptance that fate had determined they would have no future together. Vivi never came; Wolfgang never forgot or forgave her. Decades later, when my father was close to death, and I had at last met this brother, Rolf, I showed my father photos of Vivi, both as a young woman and in old age, which Rolf had brought with him. My father swept them aside with an angry motion. At the time, I did not know of the many years of anguish that had preceded this moment.

On September 26, 1949, two months after his hoped-for marriage to Vivi, Wolfgang married "the girl." I was not yet eight years old and suddenly again had a new mother—mother number three! I was present at the civil wedding, which took place in Berleburg. My father's new wife brought "the child"—my beloved sister Gisela—into my life, and for the first time I was no longer an only child.

Presumably, it was shortly before the wedding that my father introduced me to his newly intended bride, Waltraud. In order to do so, I had to travel to Berleburg by bus. I had done this a number of times before to visit my father while I was living with his parents. Few people, and certainly no one in our family, had a car. It was less than an hour's journey, but I was almost eight years old and certainly quite used to solo travel from my train days.

Chapter 26

Waltraud, Mother Number Three

WALTRAUD IRENE CONSTANZE Reuter lived with her child, Gisela, soon to become my sister, in a tiny garret over a sawmill on the perimeter of Berleburg, in circumstances well below those in which she had been raised. She was a pretty woman, twenty-seven years old, and when I compare photographs, I see significant resemblance between the two young women who played such an important role in my father's life. Their cultural backgrounds were, however, considerably different.

While Vivi's family were working class, her father having been a fireman, Waltraud's family had upper middle-class origins. She had been able to attend finishing school in the beautiful city of Freiburg in the Black Forest during 1937, followed in 1938 by six months in London in order to learn English. Her maternal grandmother was in fact British but had married a German factory owner. Waltraud's father, Max Reuter, had been a military officer during World War I who had been injured on the first day of the war, resulting in immediate release from duty. In subsequent years, he became a wine merchant, only returning to the military in 1935 due to lack of income from his chosen career. As a major, he rose to become a member of the military administration of the midsized city of Siegen in the state of Westphalia, which at that time was still part of Prussia. It was here that he died of a heart attack in 1944 while the war continued to rage. Waltraud, who had briefly worked as a volunteer, as required by law, had to arrange his cremation, including the rental of a truck to carry his body, and then obtain the coal for this procedure. These were traumatic events, especially for a young woman who had been devoted to her father. Her brother, also named Wolfgang and eleven years her senior, had already been killed in Russia in 1943, while her former boyfriend, a submarine officer, was lost at sea the same year.

The most significant name associated with the town of Siegen is Peter Paul Rubens, the Flemish painter who was born here in 1577. Although the origins of the town date to 1224, not much is left of its historic past. Because of its industries as well as the location of a crucial railroad crossing running through the town, it became the target of heavy Allied bombing. A British mission on December 16, 1944, destroyed 80 percent of the city, with fires continuing to burn for several days. Bombing continued throughout February and March 1945, with little or no resistance from the Germans.

After her father's death and the complete destruction of their home, Waltraud and her mother Maud left Siegen and moved to the sleepy town of Berleburg, lying in a very rural and forested area about thirty miles northeast. Why the choice fell on this particular community is unknown. Conjecture would lead to the fact that it was small, had no industries worth destroying, and was by this time occupied by the British. Additionally, Maud had personal contacts to the titled family, Sayn-Wittgenstein, residing in the castle of Berleburg, and my soon-to-be sister would later wear baby clothes acquired from this aristocratic family. By the time Waltraud met my father in Berleburg in April of 1946, she had indeed survived significant tragedies.

The meeting of Wolfgang and Waltraud took place at the offices of the British Control Commission. Personal goods of significant value, such as paintings, carpets, and silver had been safely stored by Waltraud's family during the war years in this area, perhaps because of Maud's connection to the aristocratic family. Since in 1946 the war was over and the region's commercial and political activities were now regulated by the British, Waltraud wished to negotiate their return. It apparently fell to my father to assist her in this process. Their attraction to each other soon resulted in a relationship during which Wolfgang asked her whether she would go to South America with him. It seems that the response was negative, as my sister Gisela was born the following year in a small town near Berleburg—and certainly still in Germany.

Chapter 27

My New Family

CHANGE WAS ONCE more imposed upon me at the age of eight as a result of my father's complicated love life. Following his marriage to his second wife, Waltraud, they established themselves in a small rental apartment in a newly developed area of Berleburg. Wolfgang continued his employment with the British Control Commission, which still had a presence there five years after the end of the war. My father had finally found a mother for his firstborn, and I was once again displaced. Some months after the wedding, I had to leave my grandparents in order to live with my new family. Again, I was enrolled in a new school, and again I had to make new friends. The year was 1950. I finally had the mother my father had so desperately sought for me, but I experienced little maternal caring from her.

Although I cannot exactly recall my emotions at this new upheaval in my life, I am certain that I was extremely saddened to leave the grandparents and the cousins I had come to love. Once again, I had no choice. It seemed that my destiny was to live with strangers, as I knew neither my father nor his new wife very well. Their expectations of me in no way took into consideration the many losses I had already sustained in my young life. I was simply absorbed. Resilience was apparently expected of me, as it had been for the general population throughout and after World War II.

In 1950, just a few short years after the end of the war, there was still much deprivation in daily life in Germany. Clothing was difficult to obtain and dresses had to be made for two growing girls, Gisela and myself. If fabric could be found at all, outfits were made in matching styles and colors for both of us. There were, in fact no, real shops in Berleburg. Wooden barracks set up in this small town had to function as such. Our toys were sparse. Amusement for me meant playing outside with neighborhood children, either with clay marbles or balls. I became quite expert at juggling a minimum of three. We jumped rope and played "heaven and hell," a game of hopscotch. During this time, I was also forced to learn how to swim. When summer arrived, I had to march each morning to the local swimming pool, quite some distance from home, no matter what the weather. Here I was attached to a long sort of fishing pole, a method by which the instructor ostensibly could prevent my drowning. I disliked these lessons intensely.

Snow was abundant in the winter of 1950, and our generous grandparents gave both my cousin Monika and me our first pair of skis for Christmas. While the landscape where I was now living presented itself as perfect for learning this new sport, my disposition did not. My feet froze in the heavy leather boots, and my father would have to thaw them in cold water on my return home. Although my cousin continued and became a fine skier, needless to say, I did not.

Only as an adult could I begin to imagine the impact my existence must have had on my new mother. She had been a young, unmarried woman, twenty-eight years old with a child aged two. Her new husband married her because the love of his life, Vivi, had not agreed to come to Germany. Additionally, Waltraud now had to assume the role of mother for a child born to yet another woman in Wolfgang's life, namely my birth mother, Helga. As a mature person I was able to understand that to be asked to love a child who has been imposed upon you, one who already has a personality and strong will, and one who does not accept you as "mother" must have been an impossible task. I felt the consequences of her inability to fabricate this love all my life, as her own children were always treated preferentially, both by her and consequently Waltraud's own mother, whom we called "Granny." It was as if a sort of revenge was being enacted upon me, who after all had been just as much a victim of my father's hasty actions and often far too slow reactions. As a child I wondered why it fell to me to polish my sister's shoes or iron her clothes. As an adult I could empathize and better comprehend my stepmother's misplaced feelings of resentment. It never changed my love for my sister Gisela nor for the sister born several years later, Marion.

It was not long before change, writ large, was once again on the horizon. This time, it did not merely involve changing locations within Germany or mothers, but actually changing countries. I had barely warmed the seat of my new school in Berleburg!

Chapter 28

We Move to England

SHORTLY AFTER MY father's marriage in September 1949, the activities of the regional office of the British Control Commission were absorbed by another region within Germany, and their offices in Berleburg closed. The British Resident Officer withdrew at the end of March 1950. My father had expected this and had applied for employment to the German Foreign Office. He was soon hired, although not within a diplomatic career path or even as a civil servant, for he did not have the requisite credentials, a university education. In the spring of 1951, he was sent to the German embassy, located in Belgravia, London, as economic secretary, a mere employee, on a trial basis.

In anticipation of yet another move, this time to a country whose language I did not know, an English tutor had been found for me in Berleburg. Regularly, after my school day at the local elementary school, and after my father's departure for England, I had to spend time with her. Perhaps I was not eager or receptive, or she was not well equipped to teach a child, but to my recollection the only phrase she managed to instill in me—never to be forgotten and never to be used—was "Take a seat, please." It amuses me still.

My father had preceded the family to London by six months during this "trial time." He took up residence in a boardinghouse in Earls Court, a district within the city. Apparently, he completed this time at the embassy successfully, as my stepmother, my sister Gisela, and I followed in October 1951, taking a train via Cologne to Hook van Holland in order to cross the English Channel. The famous spires of the Cologne Cathedral were visible from the train, rising above the rubble still remaining from the 262 separate air raids by the British on that city during World War II. More than 20,000 people died as a result of these bombings, and six years after the war it was still an endless ruin. Our ferry connection from Hook van Holland to Harwich was a lengthy overnight trip of seven hours, which left me extremely seasick. From Harwich, we proceeded by train to Liverpool Station in London, where my father was to meet us. In a traditional black London taxi we were driven to the boardinghouse. In my arms I held a favorite stuffed animal, a fox terrier I had named after a childhood novel about such a dog that I had recently read. At the time I purchased the book with my allowance, I had disappointed my father, who had hoped I would indulge in deeper literature. Having been prone to motion sickness all of my short life, I promptly became sick in the taxi and into my father's hat. It was the result of a rocky night on the ship and a subsequent breakfast of cornflakes consumed in the train's elegant, blue velvet lined dining car. I have never eaten cornflakes since.

The newly constituted Hesse family continued residing in the boardinghouse until appropriate living accommodations could be found for a more permanent residence. The smells of English breakfasts—bacon, eggs, and toast—so rare and unfamiliar to Germans at the time, has remained with me. The fact that we had to insert a shilling into the small space heater in our living quarters in order to obtain heat for an allotted time, along with other elements of a completely different way of life, are embedded memories of that relatively brief period.

Within a few weeks of our arrival in London, our parents had located a suitable flat in Ealing, a borough of London, west of the city. The house in which it was located, No. 16 Montpelier Road, was large and consisted of five generous units. It sat on a piece of land that included the terrain of a not very well-maintained lawn tennis court to one side of the building, as well as a large garden in the back. Compared to our living arrangements in Berleburg, the flat seemed gigantic. My sister Gisela and I shared a spacious bedroom with a big bay window overlooking the tennis court. In one corner was a tiny sink where we performed our morning toilette. My bed stood in an opposite corner where I considered it safe to read under the blanket by the light of my bicycle lamp at night—a forbidden pleasure. It was here and in this manner that I first devoured the novel, *Gone with the Wind*.

The apartment had one additional bedroom, one bathroom, a tiny kitchen, and what seemed to us at the time a large living-dining room. Mrs. Guernsey was hired to clean and do the laundry, which, in the absence of a washing machine, needed to be done by hand in the kitchen. On occasion, Mrs. Guernsey would stay with us when my parents traveled.

Ealing was then, and is still today, famous for the film studios where British cinema was born. It soon was to become infamous for one of the most horrific crimes ever committed there, the Montpelier Murders in 1954.

On February 11 of that year, two bodies were discovered at No. 22 Montpelier Road, in this quiet, residential area of Ealing, and just across the street from the house in which we were living, at No. 16. The address was a home for "elderly gentlefolk," was named Sunset House, and was run by the self-appointed "Lady" Mary Menzies, aged seventy-three, together with her daughter, Veronica Chesney, forty-three years old. The latter was the estranged wife of Ronald Chesney, whose real name later was revealed to be John Donald Merrett. Veronica had been poisoned with excessive gin, then drowned in a bathtub. Her mother, "Lady Menzies," had been smashed in the skull with a coffeepot and was found in an adjacent bedroom. A maid made the gruesome discovery of both bodies.

The *Ealing News* of February 11, 1954, reported that when the police arrived, they determined the women to be "quite dead"! A few days later, Chesney was also found dead, having committed suicide in a forest near Cologne, Germany. By his side lay a note addressed to his twenty-seven-year-old German mistress, Sonia, in which he claimed to be innocent of the murders but that no one would believe him. It ended Scotland Yard's manhunt for the murderer in which the German police had assisted. Later investigations revealed that Chesney, who had some years before inherited a large amount of money from an uncle, had made an insurance settlement to provide his wife an income for the rest of her life, which would revert to him on her death.

Chesney already had a colorful and criminal life behind him when these events occurred. He had been born in New Zealand in 1908 but had early in life lived in Russia. His parents brought him to Switzerland some years later, where the climate was considered to be more suitable for their child. The mother had come from a wealthy Manchester wine merchant family and wanted her son to attend university in Scotland. A brilliant mind, he nevertheless preferred a life of pleasure and decadence, forging checks on his mother's bank account to do so. When she finally discovered this on March 27, 1926, he shot her, although she did not die until two weeks later. Since there were no witnesses to the crime, the verdict on the murder charge was "not proven." For the forgery charges, he had to serve one year in prison. On his release he found refuge in the home of his mother's friend, "Lady Menzies," where he fell in love with her daughter Veronica, his later murder victim. Time spent as an officer in the Royal Navy during World War II had been for Chesney just another opportunity to continue a life of crime, smuggling drugs and arms as well as art treasures. He and his wife had become estranged by the 1950s, and it is assumed that her refusal to give him a divorce was a factor in her eventual murder.

The newspaper coverage of the "Amazing Mr. Chesney" was intense and frightened me at age twelve. Murder was not as prevalent in the news as in later years it seemed to become, or perhaps I was just too young and sheltered to understand the horrors of the wider world. Since at the time these events occurred, I had to pass this house every day on my way to school, I assiduously avoided walking on the same side of the street where the "murder home," named Sunset House, was located, and where the sun had certainly set!

Ealing's residential areas largely consisted of gracious red brick mansions, some individual homes, others divided, as was ours, into flats. There were several private schools close by, all located in what appeared to be private homes judging by their size. On what basis other than proximity my parents selected St. Michaels school for me, I cannot presume to know. It was within walking distance, classes were small (mine had ten students), and the winter uniforms were standard, forest green skirts and jumpers, tie, and white shirt. It was obligatory to wear the green felt hat, which I intensely disliked, on the way to and from

112

school. Demerits were given to students caught not complying. Classes were held around a large oval table covered with a green felt cloth. Mrs. Hicks was the principal teacher for all subjects except music. At the time, Mrs. Hicks appeared to me "old." She was a heavyset woman whom I remember only as a gray image, the color of the suit she always preferred to wear. Later, after my departure from St. Michaels, I learned that Mrs. Hicks had died in an accident with her motorcycle, from which I concluded that perhaps "old" was a relative concept, no doubt as seen from the perspective of a ten-year-old child.

It was here, and under her tutelage, that I very quickly absorbed the English language, and was shortly named to be head of my class in this subject. Additionally, my parents had registered me in elocution classes, where I was required to learn correct pronunciation and to memorize poetry, later to recite it before a board of judges. Although I never achieved recognition by way of a gold medal, my current jewelry box still contains the silver and bronze ones I was awarded by the British Poetry Society.

My first exposure to English literature occurred at St. Michaels with the reading of *A Christmas Carol* by Charles Dickens. Ever since then, I have loved this story, whether reading the book or viewing it on film. At lunchtime the felt tablecloth was removed, and the meal was served in the same space we had occupied for lessons. Roast beef with chutney was something I had never tasted before, and it quickly became my favorite meal. Music lessons were held in the basement of the building, where the triangle became my instrument of choice, or perhaps imposition, as I had no talent for any other.

But St. Michaels soon became just another brief stop in my disjointed education, as the school declared bankruptcy not long after my arrival. I was not there long enough to experience the summer uniforms.

Some distance away, and accessible only by bus, there was another private school named Wynnstay, with an equally intimate atmosphere. Beatrice Farrington was its principal. This time our winter uniforms were brown, the summer uniforms yellow gingham dresses, and the dreaded hats the same shape as at St. Michaels, round with a wide brim. In the winter, the hats were felt; in summer, straw. I quickly made friends, one of whom has remained so to this day. But as an institute of learning, it was another disastrous choice. Soon it became clear that I was not acquiring any knowledge here. As usual, I lagged behind in mathematics. Literature, to the degree that it existed here at all, interested me as I had developed a great love of reading thanks to my great-aunt. The writing of compositions also came easily to me in this newly acquired language, and I had an active imagination. But inspiration in the form of published books by well-known authors or the classics was sorely lacking.

A tiny, one-room library offered several copies of precisely two works of literature, *A Tale of Two Cities* by Charles Dickens as well as Shakespeare's *Twelfth Night*. These were read in rotation; when one was finished, we read the other, only to repeat the cycle. Religion, in those days an obligatory subject, was taught by Miss Violet Barge who read the Bible to us, word for word, and then disappeared. Miss Barge looked like the spinster she was, wearing floor-length dark dresses with her gray hair in a knot. She was a person of whom unkind young girls made fun. It appeared that she had not been trained in the subject of religion and knew only to read the printed word of the "Good Book." No discussion or explanation of a deeper meaning was ever offered. But the ultimate offense committed by this school, as far as my father was concerned, was the terrible British pronunciation of the French language that I was acquiring here. Being a linguist himself, he found this quite appalling. Not long into my tenure at Wynnstay, my parents discovered that the school was not registered with the Board of Education, whereupon I was promptly removed from it.

By now I had several years of wasted schooling behind me, a fact which was amply demonstrated when I was enrolled in yet another school in Ealing.

Although no one in our family was Catholic, my parents chose a convent school as the next experiment for my sister Gisela, now of school age, and myself. This time it was again within walking distance of our home. The school was called St. Augustine's Priory and was originally founded in Paris in 1634 as an Order for English Catholic women who wished to pursue their religious vocation. They could not do so in England, as they were being persecuted in their home country for their beliefs at that time. The Order grew rather rapidly as a center for Catholics in exile. During the French Revolution, the *dames anglaises*, as the nuns were referred to, also gave shelter to many French aristocrats. In 1904, when France passed antireligious laws, the nuns returned to England. Initially they lived in reduced circumstances in a simple house in Ealing. By 1914, they had apparently found a benefactor and were able to acquire the twelve acres on which a magnificent convent and school were constructed. It was to be the third school I would attend during my father's five-year tenure in England. The year was 1955.

As was to be expected, I again was far behind in most subjects, particularly in mathematics and chemistry; I had never acquired the basics of either and would never catch up. Nor did they interest me. In keeping with the custom of a Catholic school, a prayer was said before and after every class. In chemistry, we invoked God's help to prevent blowing ourselves up! Geography, history, particularly English history, and English literature were to remain my favorite subjects. I recall long evenings of homework, drawing precise maps showing mountain ranges, the borders of countries, and where the rivers Euphrates and Tigris flowed. I knew the names and dates of all the British kings and queens, particularly of the fascinating Tudor Period. And Alexander Pope's narrative poem, *The Rape of the Lock*, based on an actual event, was studied in detail during English literature class, as it was rumored that the young lady from whom the "lock" had been stolen had been a student of the nuns in some prior era. Whether this was in fact true is debatable, but it made the poem all the more interesting to young girls.

At St. Augustine's the uniforms were dark blue, again white shirts, dark blue hats and, worst of all, very long, dark blue 'knickers' so that during gymnastics, not a fraction other than navy blue would show as we did our various exercises. The girls in the school were divided into four houses, each named after a saint, each wearing a different color school tie for the benefit of competition between the houses. Mother Mary Gabriel, a rather young nun, was our gymnastics and sports teacher and later, long after my departure, became Mother Superior of the convent. Mother Mary Austin taught a number of the other subjects.

Although not Catholic, as a registered student I was obliged to participate in religious observances, such as during Lent, when it was our duty to attend chapel prior to classes in the mornings. As my parents did not object to this, I had no reason to consider this participation unusual. Lent necessitated "giving up something," making a sacrifice, which I chose to be remaining in bed after the alarm had sounded. For me this was a true sacrifice, but I was steadfast. The services in the chapel during those forty days of Lent consisted primarily of the recitation of the prayer "Hail Mary," and I was somewhat taken aback at the recitation of the Rosary, the repetition of this prayer, over and over again. My question to one of the nuns as to why it was not recited "once with feeling," as opposed to repeating it ten times at breakneck speed, was not met with amusement. But the nuns were caring, not inclined to punishment. They also prepared delicious meals at lunchtime, the jam tarts and rice puddings remaining among my favorite memories.

There was great emphasis on sports at St. Augustine's, and to that end we had a two-hour lunch break each day, one hour of which was required to be dedicated to one of the several sports offered. For the first time I was able to participate, playing tennis, basketball (here called netball), and field hockey on the beautiful grounds. Finally, I found myself in a real school where I quickly made new friends.

It was also at St. Augustine's that I was able to develop my early interest in acting. In July 1956 we performed _The Critic_ by Richard Sheridan. I played the main role of Mr. Puff, a playwright and critic who praises and "puffs" anything for a price.

It was likewise in Ealing that I first acquired a love of photography. For some time, I had longingly eyed a small Kodak Brownie camera in a shop window, a newly introduced model but financially beyond my means. It was therefore particularly fortuitous when, during one of my frequent bicycle trips to the local library, I found a very small coin purse lying in the street. Upon inspection I saw that it contained a one-pound note, one pound consisting of twenty shillings, the English currency at the time. Instead of continuing to the library, I quickly cycled to the local police station where I dutifully handed it over, probably much to the amusement of the policemen. I was promised that if no one claimed it within thirty days, the coin purse, including its contents, would be mine. I counted those days anxiously and was happy to go back and honestly claim this little purse. It was still not sufficient to pay for the camera, priced at twenty-four shillings, but my grandfather contributed the difference. The camera kept me company for many years, and I still have evidence of my earliest photographic achievements.

Until I was fourteen years old, my birth mother was not only an enigma but a positive unknown in my life. As I was cycled through foster mother, grandparents, and now a stepmother, I cannot recall ever giving a single thought as to who my real mother was or what she might be like. She was simply never spoken of, and I was never curious enough to ask any questions. This situation changed while we lived in England.

After the war, my natural mother Helga had married an Englishman, a soldier whom she had met in Germany, and she herself moved to England, where she gave birth to another child, again a daughter. The lack of contact was most likely due to the fact that my father had demanded of his former mother-in-law, Helga's mother, Martha Scholze, never to reveal where I was living. It was evident that he did not want me to have contact with Helga, although I was not aware of this.

The elicited promise was obviously broken, as some years later Helga located my father at the German embassy in London and expressed a desire to see me. Strangely, he agreed to the meeting, realizing perhaps that I was now old enough not to be influenced by her. The first encounter was arranged to take place in a restaurant in London. I was appalled by her appearance! Only thirty-four years old in 1955, she was extremely overweight and had obviously not paid attention to her appearance through the years of her newly married life. I have no recollection of any other aspects of this meeting or what we might have talked about. She was after all a total stranger to me, and I was at that time not interested. On returning home to my stepmother, my first question to her was "How could Dad ever have married her?"

The second and last meeting took place in our garden in Ealing. My new mother had kindly invited Helga and her little daughter Nicola, aged four at the time, ten years younger than myself, to join us for tea. During the course of this afternoon, I kept Nicola entertained, oblivious to the fact that this child was as much related to me as were my sisters Gisela and the newly born Marion. I never again thought about my birth mother until the day my second husband pondered out loud, shortly after our marriage in 1984, "I wonder how your real mother looked and how you will look when you are older!"

Chapter 29

A Detour—In Search of
My "Real Mother"

BECAUSE THERE HAD been little occasion or reason in my life to reflect on my birth mother, who, after all had never played a part in raising me, the words *real mother* meant nothing to me. I had been loved and well cared for by others. My response to my husband's musings, therefore, was that I really did not care how she looked, as I felt no respect for someone who had given away her child. All I really knew about her existence was the name of the place where she lived with her second husband and daughter. It was a small town called Deal, near Dover in the county of Kent, England. My father had once mentioned it in conversation. I had no wish to contact her and asked that my husband respect this.

But my husband was a persistent man, for despite my request and without my knowledge, he called the police department of this town and requested help in locating Mrs. Helga Smythe, her present married name, giving the reason for his search. It must have been a quiet day in Deal, the police not too occupied with excessive criminal activity at the time, as this request seemed to interest them. Within hours, an Officer Spain returned my husband's call and informed him that Mrs. Smythe was deceased, having died on June 13, 1984, less than three weeks before Syl and had I married in the Protestant church in Laasphe.

Now he felt obligated to tell me what he had done and what he had learned. I confess to a minute of emotion on hearing of my mother's death, an instinctive brief sadness—not really justified, as I had never known her. This reaction was accompanied by a moment of anger, as this reach into my past had been undertaken against my wishes. However, since the primary object of the search was no longer alive, I decided to continue this investigation and hopefully find Nicola, whom I faintly remembered as the little four-year-old girl I had played with in Ealing.

The police had advised that I contact the hospital where Helga had died in order to obtain more information. The staff at the hospital had been unaware that Mrs. Smythe had a daughter in addition to Nicola and were therefore unwilling to give me personal details as to the cause of her death. They referred me to her solicitor who, likewise, was astounded that his former client had another daughter, as he also only knew of Nicola. Although surprised and equally unwilling to impart any particulars for reasons of privacy, he instead suggested that I write Nicola a letter, which he would ensure she received. I agreed that this was a good solution. Upon receipt of my letter, he quickly forwarded it to the equally amazed Nicola, who had no idea that she had sisters. At the time she was working for ARAMCO in Saudi Arabia. Before long she contacted me by telephone, and I invited her to visit Syl and myself in the state of Vermont, where both of us were employed by the IBM Corporation, and where we had recently been civilly married.

This visit did not result in warm feelings of sisterhood. By this time, I had become curious to learn about my natural mother, Helga, from Nicky. After all, she had been raised by her and surely could tell me something about her personality, her life in England, and how she had been as a mother. But Nicky was either unwilling or unable to share any details, often stating, to my frustration, "We have no way of knowing." It was a very long month's visit with the only common denominator between us being the "unknown" we called our mother.

The primary benefit I derived from Nicky's presence was that it put me on the critical path toward learning a great deal of the history of the maternal side of my family. It is thanks to Nicky's visit that I learned that Helga's brother, our uncle Frank Scholze, was living in Karlsruhe, in Germany. He now became the most important link to the maternal side of my family.

I was not saddened at my half-sister Nicky's departure from the airport in Burlington, Vermont. Little in the way of friendship had developed between us. Upon rushing home, I immediately called Information in Karlsruhe, Germany. At the time it was the only means to locate an unknown telephone number overseas, but I was fortunate and quickly obtained it. A female voice answered at my uncle's home and responded in an unsurprised manner, as if she had been expecting my call. Jeanne, Frank's wife, casually explained that Frank was not home but was at that moment in Dresden, visiting our mother's other daughter, Klaudia. It was the very Klaudia whose fatherhood Helga had so vigorously and for so many years attempted to ascribe to Wolfgang, and which my father had equally strenuously contested. Something like the Ferchland experience had transpired in Dresden on the day I called Frank's wife. Jeanne informed me that I had been spoken about the prior evening by Frank and Klaudia, neither of them knowing of my whereabouts or whether I was even alive. The circle of my mother's three daughters was now complete, although we were not to meet for another four years, on the occasion of our uncle's sixtieth birthday in 1988.

The telephone contact with my uncle and his wife soon developed into frequent communication, primarily by way of letters. Frank now became the conduit from which flowed all the subsequent information pertaining to the maternal side of my family. Strangely, now that my mother was dead, my interest in her had become alive!

Chapter 30

Helga Scholze, My "Real Mother"

MY BIRTHMOTHER, HELGA, was born on February 21, 1921, in Berlin, the oldest child of Paul and Martha Scholze. For seven years, she was the "princess" in the household. According to my uncle Frank, her brother, extreme rivalry and jealousy, eventually culminating in animosity, developed on Helga's part when Frank, the longed-for-son was born on October 23, 1928. She was no longer the center of attention. Helga carried this resentment throughout her life, poisoning their relationship.

She was an extremely intelligent child, clever at imitating people, particularly the voices of movie stars, and developed a fine ear for languages. For a period of time Helga attended school in Sweden while living with her aunt, her mother's sister. Frank writes that she was always a difficult person, demanding and angry that her father did not provide the lifestyle she wanted and felt she deserved. In a letter in my possession, written by her mother on the occasion of her sixteenth birthday in 1937, she reprimands her daughter severely for her unpleasant attitude and behavior, pointing out that her father had always provided well for them and that she had never lacked for anything.

Helga aged 1½ years with her mother Martha Scholze

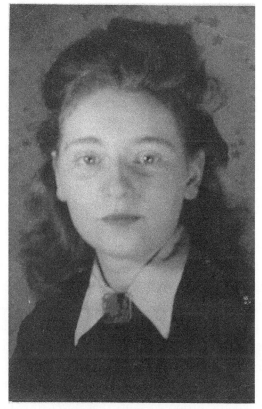

My mother Helga ca.1945

Having been divorced from my father in 1944, Helga met her future husband, Walter Smythe, a Royal Artillery sergeant, on a train platform in Berlin in 1946. She was at that time twenty-five years old. By June 1947, Helga was on her way to England, via Frankfurt and Amsterdam, traveling in an American four-engine airplane in order to marry him. On the evening of her arrival, sixteen million subscribers were able to read in both the London *Evening News* and *Evening Star* about a "pretty, golden-haired" German, Miss Helga Hesse, who had arrived at Croyden Airport in London without a penny in her pocket—and no fiancé to meet her. A miscommunication had sent him to the Dutch Airline Terminal in Sloane Square to await her arrival. The headline in the *Evening Star* of June 27, 1947, read, "Helga arrives without money, her fiancé is not there." Walter had sent Helga the money for her flight, but how the press came to learn of her arrival, I do not know.

Soon Walter and Helga were officially engaged. For the occasion, Helga received "a gold ring with 5 diamonds, 3 pairs of shoes, stockings, a pullover and a long green jacket." In August 1947, they were married. Coming from postwar Germany, Helga must have believed that she had arrived in paradise. She finally felt like a "human being again" and in subsequent letters to friends, Helga writes in glowing terms about life in England.

Helga and Walter had agreed that they did not want children "because one could not have a life and would be tied down." In a letter to a friend, Helga expressed that she had experienced what it was like to have an "unwanted baby," undoubtedly referring to my birth in 1941 in Berlin. In a subsequent letter, this time referencing Klaudia's birth, she wrote that she had to keep the fact of Klaudia's existence from her new husband forever. "Walter is marrying me and not my past," she explained. Helga had also left this child with foster parents, this time with friends of her parents in Dresden, and consequently, as with me, an older generation. I possess copies of dozens of letters written to her younger daughter, Klaudia, both immediately after her arrival in England and in years to come. Assumedly they were kept secret from her new husband. Many of these letters promised Klaudia gifts that never arrived and proposed visits that never took place. Whether Walter was ever made aware of *my* existence I do not know. Given that Nicola, the daughter she apparently had not wanted either, did not know that she had half-sisters, it is doubtful that Walter even knew that his German wife had been married before.

Thirteen years later Helga was less enthusiastic, and indeed unhappy, about her life in England. In April 1960, she wrote to a previous employer in Berlin enquiring about the possibility of obtaining work, to which she received a negative reply. In a German newspaper article, dated September 13, 1960, a glaring headline reports: "The English are too unfriendly—Berlin War Bride wants to return after 13 years, her British husband will accompany her." My mother is quoted in the article as being "extremely disappointed," that while the English were always polite, they were never friendly, and no one ever came to visit her. She felt that whenever she entered a shop, conversation would stop, and that people would talk about her behind her back. Quoted in the same article are the words of another German immigrant, living in the same town, who had experienced just the opposite, having made many English friends.

Helga with new husband, Walther Smythe, 1947

Helga now believed she could only be happy again if she returned to Berlin. But the permanent return never came about, and only occasional visits to Germany occurred. In August 1986, her brother, my uncle Frank, wrote that Helga was torn all her life. "She was always a good German in England and a good Englishwoman in Germany. She was never content." The siblings had never had a good relationship. To quote Frank, Helga was "like a volcano, one was never certain what would happen next." In her final years, my mother again had disagreements with her brother, and they communicated only through her attorney. By 1984, the year my husband voiced his curiosity, my mother was dead.

Chapter 31

Frank Scholze, Helga's Brother

UNCLE FRANK HAD been an actor all his life. As a young man, while still living in Berlin, he performed in films and on the radio. Later in his career and for several decades until his death, he was an actor-in-residence at the well-known State Theatre of Karlsruhe. He had married Jeanne von Reckow, a ballerina from Alsace, who early in her dancing life, suffered injuries severe enough to prevent the continuation of her chosen career. She subsequently became a professional photographer. They had one daughter named Saskia, whom I also met for the first time in 1988, thereby adding another cousin to my life.

It was from Uncle Frank that I learned of the turbulent and historically significant role his father and my maternal grandfather, Paul Scholze, who eventually became a leading Communist, played in Germany in the early part of the twentieth century. Frank saw his father for the last time when he was less than five years old, so he never really knew him. When he was a young adult, his mother Martha, would have been the primary source of information concerning her husband's political activism. She knew quite soon after his death that Paul Scholze had lost his life in Russia but only suspected the actual circumstances of how this occurred. It was not until the Fall of the Berlin Wall in 1989, and the reunification of East and West Germany, that these suspicions were confirmed. By then, Martha Scholze, who had remarried in the interim, was also dead.

Frank Scholze, actor and uncle, 1954

Part 3

The Tumultuous Maternal Side

Chapter 32

Paul Scholze, Political Activist

PRIOR TO 1983, historians in Germany had begun research in order to document the biographies of certain individuals, men and women, who had been persecuted, imprisoned or murdered by the Nazis on the basis of their political beliefs or activities. The turbulence of reunification put a temporary halt to this research. However, the "Fall of the Wall" in 1989 brought with it the benefit of the sudden availability of new material, both from the archives of the former East Germany and from Russia, and even from individual families' personal histories. Of the over four hundred biographies being considered for special recognition, thirty-two were chosen for the publication of a book entitled *Vor die Tuer Gesetzt*—loosely translated as "kicked out the door." It is a compilation of the lives of members of the Berlin City Council, as well as Berlin Magistrates, who had been persecuted by the National Socialists. These thirty-two individuals, both men and women, were chosen on the basis of their particularly interesting lives and destinies. My grandfather, Paul Scholze, was among them. The book was also the basis for an accompanying exhibition held from September through November of 2005 in the famous Red City Hall of Berlin Schoeneberg, the very city hall where my own birth had been registered. Although unable to attend its opening, I was invited to view the smaller but permanent portion of the exhibit, which included that pertaining to my grandfather, at a later date.

The historians and authors of the book, who were also the organizers of the exhibition, personally guided me through it. It was a strange and curious experience to be facing a greatly enlarged photographic portrait of the grandfather I had never known, when I entered the beautiful old Red City Hall in Berlin, this symbolic red brick structure with its marvelous stained-glass windows, which my grandfather had frequented while serving on the City Council. Within the exhibition rooms stood tall glass cases, one of which was dedicated to Paul Scholze and his family. It contained documents pertaining to his life and photographs of his—and consequently my—family: my maternal grandmother and their children, my uncle Frank and my birth mother Helga.

Uncle Frank had independently decided to write about his father and had made contact with a prominent German historian who assisted him greatly in his research. Since Russian archives were now available following 'Reunification', it was possible to reconstruct Paul Scholze's final years. In 2004 his political life had also been included in a volume entitled "Germany's 400 Most Important Communists: A Biographical Handbook", spanning the years 1918 to 1945. He is mentioned in most history books and articles documenting social movements to improve workers' rights in the early twentieth century in Germany. Many of these Communists, including my grandfather, had been members of the Berlin City Council or the Judiciary.

A television series of Paul Scholze's life had been in the planning stages when my uncle unfortunately suffered a stroke at age sixty-three. It caused him to be wheelchair-bound on the fourth floor of a building, which had no elevator, in Karlsruhe, thereby severely restricting his life. It put an end to his writing but not to his interest in the subject. Before his death in 2008 at age eighty, Frank had sent me copies of all his research material concerning his father, including books that referenced him, and a great number of family photographs. Since I was the only one of his nieces interested in the story, it has fallen to me to document the important contributions my maternal grandfather made in his objective to improve the lives of Germany's working class at the beginning of the twentieth century.

I believe that Paul Scholze was born with revolution churning in his veins. His birth took place on April 13, 1886, in the city of Dresden in

Saxony. Photographs of him as a young man show him to be slim and relatively slight in stature, with dark hair and a mustache. Not at all the image of a man who would help shape history. Of course, photos could not project the force of his personality. His demeanor did not foretell the revolutionary within!

In the decades prior to Paul Scholze's birth, social unrest in a number of European countries, including Germany, had finally developed into revolution in 1848. Initiated by street demonstrations of French workers seeking improvement in working conditions, freedom of assembly and the press, as well as greater liberties in general, it led to the abdication of King Louis Philippe I of France in February of that year. By March, this movement had spread to neighboring Germany, where diverging factions had a variety of different goals in mind. Among the working class, the unrest manifested itself initially less politically than socially. There were, of course, demands for improved working conditions and wages, but there were also peasant insurrections and artisan riots. Liberals called for greater economic freedom, and nationalists demanded unification of the country.

Germany was at that time a federation of thirty-nine sovereign states, each having its own king or grand duke, each having its own constitution, governing system, and laws. In short, there was a general call for democratic reforms on many levels. While the revolution as a whole failed, some concessions were made by the existing government. A document of fundamental rights was published in December of 1848 in which it was agreed that there should be one federal state with an emperor. But it was not until 1871 that the Prussian, Prince Otto von Bismarck, was able to bring this about at the end of the Franco-Prussian War. He also continued to promote social reforms by way of seeking improvement of conditions for the working class, creating social insurance and instituting "the world's first welfare state."[17] In spite of these positive changes, great social inequality remained.

A Social Workers' Party calling itself the SPD (Socialist Party of Germany), which aimed to spread socialist principles, had been founded in 1869 by Wilhelm Liebknecht and August Bebel but was banned by 1878. Due to continued popular support however, it was again legalized in 1890. Subsequently the party was represented in the

German Reichstag (Parliament) and by 1912 was the strongest political party in Germany. In the following years, the most comprehensive system of social insurance in Europe was enacted by the SPD. The party exists to this day, although much diminished in influence and changed in its focus.

This was the political and social climate into which my grandfather was born to parents who were themselves Social Democrats and members of the SPD party. They were working class people, his father, Adolph Scholze, being a toolmaker. Paul, after completion of his schooling at age fourteen and subsequent training, followed his father in this trade in 1900 when he was sixteen years old. He became involved in the socialist movement from the earliest, and as a result, it was almost a given that this political orientation would dictate his life and career. While still in the second year of his apprenticeship in 1901, he had already been disciplined by his employer for participation in a May Day parade, this being the International Worker's Day, which celebrated workers' rights and the eight-hour workday. By 1902, he had joined a union and so began a career attempting to improve conditions for the working man.

Although I never knew my maternal grandfather, as he died some years before my birth, his life and activities are abundantly documented for me to realize that Paul Scholze was a force of nature, a person of strong will and character, most particularly when it involved social issues.

Following completion of his apprenticeship as a toolmaker, Paul worked for nine months, then began life as a "journeyman." This is a very old German custom in which trained workers travel throughout the country, practicing their trade and counting on the help and generosity of the public for survival. It is still practiced in some parts of Germany today. In some cases, a journeyman's travels may last for several years. During his time in that capacity, Paul participated in strikes and lockouts of metal workers in various cities throughout the country, returning to Dresden in 1904. At the age of eighteen, Paul officially joined the SPD party. It had by then become the largest political party in Germany and continued for decades to play a strong role in shaping life for the working class in the early part of the twentieth century.

As a result of his participation in the strikers' movement, Scholze was soon blacklisted, not just in Dresden but in the entire state of Saxony, making it impossible to find employment. Consequently, he left for Prague and later to Vienna, Austria, which was German-speaking and part of the Austro-Hungarian Empire. Here he not only found work, but he also switched to the Austrian metalworkers' union. He joined the Austrian Socialist Party and again took part in strikes and demonstrations, fighting in that country for the right to vote, as well as being involved in general organizational activities. Eventually, the Austrians also had enough of Paul Scholze and threatened him with deportation. As a result, he returned to Germany, specifically Berlin, voluntarily. He was now faced with imminent military duty, and while this was temporarily postponed, he used the intervening time to continue his participation in metalworkers' strikes, most particularly targeting munition manufacturers.

My grandfather's personality apparently embodied leadership qualities and created trust in others, for he was elected by his peers and coworkers to most of the subsequent positions he held throughout his life. He was chosen to become an intermediary agent in union negotiations and a shop steward and was among the district leadership of the metalworkers' union and its agitation committees in various companies. Additionally, Paul Scholze became a member of the extended town administration and executive committee for a social-democratic borough within the city limits of Berlin. These activities often resulted in disciplinary action and frequent unemployment; he endured short prison terms and frequent fines.

At age twenty-two, in the autumn of 1908, my grandfather joined the 50th Infantry Regiment to serve two years of duty in the German army. Even while in the military, he was involved in repeated political conflicts, although as punishment he was usually subjected only to harassment and relatively mild discipline. By April 1910, he was released due to illness.

In 1911, Paul was once more living in Berlin and had begun work for the munitions plant, Knorr-Brakes, which, in addition to military weapons, also manufactured railway braking systems. He again began to agitate for improved working conditions as he quickly became a member of the German Metalworkers Union and later a union official. Drafted into the military once more, both in 1914 as well as in 1915, he was released from duty each time due to a continuing heart problem and was finally declared medically unfit to serve. This did not prevent him from devoting his energies to continued union activities and particularly strikes against the armaments industry. One police document states that his employer would be most happy to be rid of Scholze, as well as two equally disruptive coworkers. In the event, not enough evidence existed to legally prosecute these men as criminals.

In his book *The German Revolution, 1917–1923*, Pierre Broue writes: "These metalworkers were certainly the finest people in Social Democracy and in the pre-war trade union movement. Unknown in 1914, by the end of the war they were to be the accepted leaders of the workers in Berlin and, despite their relative youth, the cadres of the revolutionary socialist movement. The majority ... became Communists in 1919/1920 and were close to the Spartacists such as Paul Eckert and Paul Scholze."[18]

In addition to his union agitation, my grandfather had become a member of a commission for the protection of children in several social-democratic voting districts in the city of Berlin and later, in 1916, was elected auditor for the central voting committees of these districts.

In 1914, the Social Democratic Party of Germany (SPD), headed by Chancellor Friedrich Ebert, was the majority party with a 35 percent share of the votes in Parliament. Paul Scholze had been born into a family that supported its policies. When Germany invaded Russia in August 1914, thereby instigating World War I, the party, although supporting the war itself, was divided as to the authorization of funding for this endeavor. Europe at this time consisted of many complex alliances, and there were multiple reasons for Germany's involvement in a war for which all European countries had been preparing for years, each with their own objectives. The assassination of the Archduke Ferdinand, heir to the Austrian throne and an ally of Germany, was the precipitating event.

Germany considered it a war of defense and although the SPD party members were largely in support, among the general population and particularly among the shop stewards representing the munitions industry, there was soon a growing resentment to the many deaths at the front, while at the same time there were growing social needs at home.

At the beginning of the war, there had been relatively little dissent within the population as a whole, as the public initially believed that it would end quickly. They were confident of victory. This confidence soon changed quite dramatically, primarily due to "a progressive deterioration of living standards for the vast majority of the population."[19] The process leading to the starvation of the population had been set in motion by the naval blockade referred to earlier and that had been enacted by the British in 1914. It was to last for the duration of the war. Germany not only quickly ran short of food and clothing, but it was soon suffering famine, the price of food in some instances having risen by 50 percent. Workers became resentful, especially since this deprivation was not equally shared by the population. The anger against this inequity manifested itself against the wealthy, military officers, factory and shop owners, and businessmen, who became the objects of hatred. It was fertile ground for political opposition and strikes.

By August 1914, revolutionary elements had already developed within the SPD party, leading to the creation of a radical splinter group calling itself the Spartacus League, named after the leader of a slave rebellion during the Roman Republic. Their tactics included agitating among German workers by way of strikes and leading antiwar marches, urging them to turn against the government. The League had been founded by Karl Liebknecht, son of the founder of the SPD party, and Rosa Luxemburg, a Polish-born lawyer, Marxist, and antiwar activist. Karl Liebknecht had been a member of the German Parliament, and the *only* member who had voted against the war.

As a result of his own leftist and antiwar activities, Paul Scholze had come into contact with both Liebknecht and Luxemburg. Like them, he participated in illegal antiwar demonstrations and was heavily involved in the preparation and creation of antiwar material. Both Liebknecht and Luxemburg spent the majority of World War I in prison due to their membership in the Spartacus League and their opposition to the war. Paul's future wife, Martha Eschbach, my grandmother-to-be, had also befriended Rosa and visited her in prison. During her incarceration, Rosa showed a less political and confrontational side of her personality, writing charming letters to Sonja, the wife of Karl Liebknecht, describing her daily routine in prison and the books she read, quoting poetry she had memorized, and naming the birds she was able to identify from her prison window. In spite of her own difficult circumstances, the letters are exceedingly positive and hopeful in tone and are intended to alleviate the anxiety Liebknecht's wife surely was experiencing as a result of her husband's imprisonment. These letters have been compiled into a small volume entitled *Rosa Luxemburg's Letters from Prison.*

Chapter 33

Paul Scholze, Revolutionary

IN 1916, A more radical wing of the SPD Party had been formed, calling itself the USPD (Independent SPD). Paul Scholze's involvement with it began soon thereafter. By 1917, this group had more than a hundred thousand members, and my grandfather, at that time, had no reason to join the previously formed and even more radical Spartacus League. But even within the USPD the goals were not uniformly held. There were those who wanted a revolution, while others preached moderation in the hope of reform by the government in power.

Paul Scholze was at this time again employed and continuing his agitation activities at Knorr-Brakes where he was one of seventeen hundred workers. He had recently published a leaflet entitled *In which direction are free unions being forced?* The authorities claimed that with its publication he was injecting disharmony into the workplace—disharmony that in fact had already long existed between the two political factions, SPD and USPD. Management at Knorr-Brakes feared that unless Scholze was removed from the company as quickly as possible, there was danger of a "solidarity strike."

He was accused of being a member of the "modern workers' movement" and a subscriber to a newspaper called *Vorwaerts* (Forward), the central organ of the Social Democratic Party, which had been in existence since 1876. Originally it had favored pacifism and neutrality, but by 1916, it took an antiwar position and was consequently forbidden.

While the war was ongoing, Scholze had become a member of the "Revolutionary Stewards," who were independently chosen by workers in various German industries. The Stewards were among those, who within the Independents wing of the SPD, the USPD, supported opposition to the war and were most heavily represented in the armaments industry. As a result of my grandfather's frequent participation in strikes, he came under police surveillance.

The Berlin police president characterized Paul Scholze in a report dated April 19, 1917, in the following manner: "He belongs to the most radical elements of the Social Democratic workers movement. Wherever it is possible he attempts to create dissatisfaction and to develop subversive activities."

Certainly, there was another strike being planned at Knorr-Brakes at this time. In early April 1917, the Spartacists, with the agreement of the USPD, had distributed leaflets calling for mass protests. Among the workers' demands were the following:

1. Release Karl Liebknecht, who had been arrested for treason and received a prison sentence of four years, for his participation in a demonstration against the war
2. Release all currently imprisoned participants in the workers movement
3. Allow complete freedom in all political development
4. Provide adequate supply of food
5. End the war without reparation demands or occupation of foreign territory

A committee was formed at Knorr-Brakes with the purpose of requesting a meeting with Friedrich Ebert, who headed the SPD and was one of the leaders of the Parliament, in order to present these demands. This request was denied, and instead the committee was referred to an undersecretary. Meanwhile, a secret vote had determined that workers should continue to strike. On April 16, 1917, employees at three hundred firms went on strike, among them Knorr-Brakes. "These strikers had decided to put the demand for Liebknecht's release at the head of their ultimatums. A worker's council had been elected over which the revolutionary Paul Scholze presided, and who in turn called for such a council to be elected in every armaments factory."[20] These council members were intended to be the only ones to negotiate with the government. Knorr-Brakes' workers elected three people to their council, the first among them being Paul Scholze. Unfortunately, the chosen three were the main agitators at the plant. But the military intervened, the striking workers were disciplined, and the three leaders, Paul Scholze among them, were arrested. The head of the armaments section of the military's general staff appealed to the patriotism of the workers by writing, "Our worst enemies are in our midst ... the agitators for strikes—whoever goes on strike when our armies are facing the enemy is a cur."[21]

In a document dated April 22, 1917, my grandfather reported that Berlin had just experienced a massive strike with the participation of over three hundred thousand people. He called upon workers in all parts of the country to remain active in the movement. Not only were the strikers' demands related to work conditions, but he also called for the proletariat to take the "freedom movement" into their own hands and to reject "imperialism."

The strikers wanted an end to the war, a just peace agreement with Russia, and assurance that the German empire would not claim Russian territory. None of these demands were met by the government.

In January 1918, a new strike was proposed by an action committee consisting of eleven members, which comprised the nucleus of the revolutionaries, among them Paul Scholze. This time the demands included the representation of workers in the peace negotiations, an improved supply of food, freedom of expression, restricted child labor, universal suffrage at age twenty, as well as an end to military control of factories. The undersecretary had agreed to meet representatives of the committee but upon their arrival decided he would receive only two members. Consequently, Paul Scholze and another deputy decided to remain in the waiting room, while the two chosen representatives attempted to negotiate these demands. The results of the meeting were that the action committee was declared to be illegal, potentially leading to criminal proceedings.

Continued illegal protest activities, numerous arrests, and subsequent releases—both from employment and from prison terms—followed, only strengthening my grandfather's leftist political leanings and resolve. His contact with the Spartacus League within the USPD now grew. He was named chairman of the Central Commission for Strike Leadership as they prepared for the beginning of another munitions workers' strike. The strike ended with Paul Scholze again being drafted and in early 1918 being sent to Verdun, which in 1916 had been the scene of one of the fiercest and most bloody battles of the war. While there, he was once more arrested, and a war tribunal was initiated against him. It was never carried out due to lack of evidence and the silence maintained by other participants.

The terrible working conditions during the winter of 1917–18 eventually mobilized even those who had up to now distanced themselves from any antiwar movements. In ever greater numbers they demanded removal of the military dictatorship. January 28, 1918 was the first day of the largest mass strike to occur in Western Europe since the beginning of the war, with at least four hundred thousand workers participating. They were partially inspired by the success of the Bolshevik Revolution in Russia under the Communists Lenin and Trotsky. Their demands again included an immediate end to the war, a "just peace" with Russia and without territorial demands or annexation, sufficient food supply, freedom of the press, and total democratization of all state institutions. The most immediate targets of these strikes were always munitions manufacturers. They were the capitalists who received supplies, among them copper and grenade fuses from enemy countries such as England and France, which were used to manufacture weapons that in turn killed German soldiers. In total over one million workers demonstrated for an end to the massacre. Their demands were not met; some factories received military protection, and many of the strikers were subsequently forced into military service.

The Revolutionary Stewards, my grandfather among them, had for some time been calling for an end to the monarchy. Public pressure for the abdication of the emperor, Wilhelm II of Prussia, had also been strong for a considerable period of time, although he had staunchly resisted it. While the country stood on the threshold of yet another revolution and a new antiwar strike, planned for November 9, 1918, the emperor's abdication was finally announced on this very day, although before he had actually consented to it. He subsequently fled to Holland, where he lived out his life until 1941. Wilhelm II would be the last German emperor. In his inherited royal position, he had been the head of the government, a role that now went to Friedrich Ebert, who, as leader of the SPD Party, became Germany's first president. Philipp Scheidemann, a member of this party and one of its ministers, proclaimed the first German Republic that very same November day of 1918 by giving a spontaneous speech that closed with the following words: "The old and rotten, the monarchy has collapsed. The new may live. Long live the German Republic!"

The armistice ending World War I was signed on November 11, 1918, two days after the emperor's abdication. Although Ebert, in his new position as head of the government, attempted to consolidate and share power with the various factions of SPD and USPD, no consensus could be reached as to how a future government should be structured. Fighting and skirmishes continued and were additionally provoked by an earlier event on October 28, 1918, when "sailors of the Imperial Navy at Kiel disobeyed orders to put to sea."[22] They knew that the end of the war was near and refused to put their lives on the line for what they "considered to be a suicidal mission against the British fleet."[23] Government troops were deployed against these mutineers. The head of the Berlin police department, Emil Eichhorn, himself a member of the USPD, the more radical faction within the SPD, was dismissed due to his refusal to take action against the sailors' mutiny during the Christmas holidays, referring to it as "Ebert's bloody Christmas."

The revolutionaries had considered Eichhorn to be the last independent and honest man still in a powerful position in Germany and resisted his expulsion. In spite of the many political differences among the USPD, the Shop Stewards, and the Spartacists, in this climate of rage they united in calling for mass protests and demonstrations in support of Eichhorn who was being slandered by the government. The contagion spread from port to port as well as to inland cities. Factory workers were infuriated, and members of the Home Army participated in the demonstrations. The leader of the Shop Stewards in Germany,

Richard Mueller, declared that "Germany was a tinder box waiting for a match."[24] Revolutionary soldiers and workers believed that the Ebert government had betrayed them and needed to go.

Friedrich Ebert would be among the leaders of the Social Democrats who helped create the Constitution of the Weimar Republic in an attempt to unite the country. It was formally announced on August 11, 1919, although political turmoil continued in the coming years. Ebert resigned in 1923 and died in 1925. It was his successor, Paul von Hindenburg, a former general and statesman, who, under pressure from the right wing, named Adolf Hitler as Chancellor, thereby paving the way for the Nazi's assumption of power in 1933.

Chapter 34

Paul Scholze Becomes a Communist

MY GRANDFATHER HAD by this time also become a member of the extreme left and the radical Spartacus League. Among them there was a strong push to form an independent party. Although Rosa Luxemburg had been a founding member of the league, she was against such a formation and especially against calling it, as proposed, a Communist Party. She felt it would frighten people. But with Lenin's encouragement from afar in Russia, and a subsequent vote within the central committee of the Spartacus League, it was agreed that a new party should be formed. Consequently, on December 30, 1918, they voted to establish the German Communist Party with the support of not only the Spartacists but also the Free Socialist Youth Organization and the International Communist Party. My grandfather was now officially a Communist!

On January 6, 1919, Paul Scholze, as representative of the Revolutionary Shop Stewards, Karl Liebknecht for the Communist Party, and Georg Ledebour, a journalist and member of the USPD, created and issued a Manifesto stating that the Ebert Government had been deposed and that they, the Revolutionary Committee, representing "Revolutionary Socialist workers and Soldiers, the Independent Socialist Party and the Communist Party" would temporarily take over the Government. The actual wording of the Manifesto, as translated by the Avalon Project at Yale Law School reads as follows:

COMRADES! WORKERS!

The Ebert-Scheidemann Government has rendered itself impossible. It is hereby declared deposed by the undersigned Revolutionary Committee, the Representative of the Revolutionary Socialist Workers and Soldiers, Independent Social Democratic Party and Communist Party.

The undersigned Revolutionary Committee has provisionally assumed the conduct of the business of government.

COMRADES! WORKERS!

Support the measures of the Revolutionary Committee. Berlin, January 6, 1919

The Revolutionary Committee

George Ledebour, Karl Liebknecht, Paul Scholze

The wording of the document clearly evidences that the three men were merely signing as representatives of the Committee, that their "takeover" was provisional. It did not suggest that they would be the future government, although that is how it was interpreted. Liebknecht, having acted impulsively, did not have the authority of his party to issue such a document and Rosa Luxemburg, although a founder of the Spartacus League and a Communist herself, recently released from prison, was not in agreement with this declaration. She refused to put her signature to it, although that did not prevent the government from arresting her and Liebknecht and shortly murdering both.

The document asked "comrades and workers" to join the cause and called for mass demonstrations in Berlin. The following day more than two hundred thousand demonstrators took to the streets, among them weaponized members of the Spartacus League. Workers occupied many public facilities in the capital, including newspaper and book publishing houses; the headquarters of *Forward*, the paper to which my grandfather had subscribed and for which he occasionally wrote articles; food warehouses, and railroad stations.

Meanwhile, the members of the Revolutionary Committee met and consulted, throughout the day and the night. No one had any clear idea as to how to proceed. There was talk of arresting the members of the Cabinet and arming the workers, but there was confusion and lack of leadership within their ranks. Long speeches were held but no plan, no strategy was presented as to what to do next. Even Rosa Luxemburg stated that the leadership had failed, although she later supported their actions.

The insurrections resulted in heavy fighting between citizens and government troops. None of the reinforcements the revolutionaries had expected arrived. At least 165 people were killed. The assembled masses grew restless, became disillusioned, and eventually returned to their homes. The uprising was quickly crushed by the military between January 9 and 12, 1919.

The Ebert government responded to this attempted coup with the help of what remained of the military following the end of the war, as well as with the *Freikorps* (Free Corps), which consisted primarily of paramilitary groups and military volunteers. Mostly these were disaffected men who were angry about losing the war and wanted revenge against the Communists. Nationalist and patriotic, most of these men were unemployed. Many of them later ended up in Hitler's National Socialist (Nazi) Party.

The minister of defense, Gustav Noske, was ordered by Ebert to return peace to the capital of Berlin. He accepted this duty by stating, "Well, somebody has to be the bloodhound," and employed the above groups to murder both Rosa Luxemburg and Karl Liebknecht on January 15, 1919. Luxemburg's body was thrown into the Landwehr Canal, which flows through Berlin, not to be recovered until five months later. Both are considered to be martyrs of the German Left movement.

Ledebour was arrested on January 9 and taken into custody. During a trial in May 1919, in which he was defended by the murdered Karl Liebknecht's brother Theodor, he stated that he took full responsibility

GABRIELE H. MINITER

for the revolutionary actions of the workers against the government because "he considered it necessary to rid the country of the criminal government as quickly as possible in the interest of workers as well as of the entire population."[25] Theodor Liebknecht's defense caused Ledebour to be exonerated on May 20, 1919. Meanwhile, in anticipation of high fines, it was suggested by the Committee and Party leadership that Paul Scholze should become "illegal"—that is to say, go underground. Although he left Berlin, he continued to be involved in antigovernment activity in other German cities. A suit of high treason had been brought against him in 1920 in conjunction with his signature of the manifesto proposing to oust the Ebert government. It was later terminated through a court decision, permitting his return to Berlin.

By 1919, the Spartacus League had renamed itself the Communist Party of Germany. My grandfather had become active in the conversion movement of members of the USPD, the Independent SPD, having himself become a Communist Party member and a delegate to their first Party Day on October 19, 1920. It was held in the old university city of Halle, where my paternal grandfather, Walther Hesse, had studied law. Today it lies in the state of Saxony-Anhalt, which until 1989 remained within the borders of Communist Germany. In March and April 1920, Paul Scholze continued to participate in some of the most brutal and bloody uprisings in Germany, particularly in the heavy industrialized areas of the Ruhr. Beginning as a radical putsch against the Ebert government, it turned into a violent strike among the workers whose participants, about eighty thousand strong, were called the Red Ruhr Army. Paul Scholze was one of the organizers. A photograph taken in March 1920, later reprinted in books and journals documenting the events, shows him standing beside a machine gun while its potential use was being demonstrated. By early April, the strike had been put down by the government, but not before many were killed. Men were dragged from their homes, and shirts were torn off their backs. Any pressure marks on their bodies presumed that the individual had carried a rifle and they were immediately shot. Even girls and women who had offered their services as paramedics or kitchen helpers were ruthlessly killed. All were buried in mass graves.

150

In later years it was speculated that, had the Social Democratic movement remained united and stronger, as opposed to splintering into several factions, much agony would have been spared the world in that it might have prevented the rise of Hitler, the Third Reich, and World War II.

Paul Scholze continued to participate all over Germany in the interest of Spartacus groups and the left wing of the USPD. He organized, he spoke, and he became a delegate to various Party functions. By 1921, he was responsible for the political and military work of the Communist Party of Germany. In order to gain more experience, he went to the Soviet Union in March 1921, returning to Berlin several months later. Following his return, and at the request of the Communist Party Central Committee, he went to the region of Silesia, an area within Prussia that today lies primarily in Poland, as Party Secretary, in order to lead another large miners' strike. Approximately thirty thousand men participated. But my grandfather's strike-leading days were coming to an end, as other opportunities in the fight for social justice opened to him.

Chapter 35

Martha Scholze

WHILE PAUL SCHOLZE'S early years of political and revolutionary involvement are heavily documented, there is never any mention of his personal life. When he married Martha Frieda Franziska Eschbach on July 20, 1921, in Berlin, she is referred to as his second wife. Their daughter, my future birth mother Helga, had already been born in February of that year. There is no record of who his first wife might have been. Paul and Martha's wedding license states that neither had a religious affiliation, as eventually neither would their two children, my uncle Frank or my mother, Helga.

Like her new husband, Paul Scholze, Martha had been born into a family of Social Democrats on May 9, 1895, in Berlin. Her father, Hermann Eschbach, was involved in establishing food cooperatives and was employed as a warehouse keeper. These cooperatives, originally created in England, served the needs of the poor working population, many of whom had moved to the cities from the countryside in order to find work. They were often abused by ruthless landlords and cheated in food shops, where they were sold products of poor and often spoilt quality at high prices. Frequently consumers became indebted to the shop owners as a result of buying on credit, adding to the misery of their already difficult lives. These cooperatives were usually created in industrialized areas at the initiative of socially minded citizens or unions in conjunction with the growing numbers of workers and political movements.

On completion of her schooling in Berlin Schoeneberg, Martha trained as a stenographer and typist, her first positions being in law offices. At the age of eighteen in 1913, she not only joined the SPD party but also participated in educational courses of the Workers Movement. On May 1, 1916, she had taken part in the first real antiwar demonstrations, which occurred on the Potsdamer Platz in Berlin. In keeping with her own political views, from 1918 and continuing through the time of the Revolution in 1919, she worked as secretary to Paul Eckert, who headed the Workers and Soldiers Executive Council of Greater Berlin. It was here that she first crossed paths with Paul Scholze.

Martha (Eschbach) Scholze, future maternal grandmother, 1918

Martha and Paul Scholze, 1920

Chapter 36

Paul Scholze and the IAH

PAUL'S INVOLVEMENT WITH issues for social justice had taken a different turn in 1920, when he came into contact with Willi Muenzenberg. The latter had been born into poverty in 1889 in the town of Erfurt, Thuringia, where Martin Luther, "Father of the Protestant Reformation," had been ordained in 1507 and where he later lived as a monk. Muenzenberg's life took a path similar to that of my grandfather. During a 2018 visit to the Cathedral of St. Mary in Erfurt, which had been in the Russian zone until Reunification in 1989, I found myself studying with interest a plaque in memory of Willi Muenzenberg. At that time, I was not aware of who he was or of Paul Scholze's association with him. I did not know of the impact this man had on my grandfather's life. Not until later did I learn that he, just as my grandfather, had early in life become active in trade unions and was likewise originally a member of the SPD. When the party split, forming the more radical USPD, Muenzenberg, like Paul Scholze, followed this wing. In the years 1919 to 1920, he was the first head of the Young Communist International.

During World War I, Muenzenberg frequently visited Lenin, the founder of the Russian Communist Party, who was living in exile in Switzerland, following his participation in antitsar protests and the revolution, which caused the tsar's abdication. Lenin had recognized Muenzenberg's organizing skills, and in spite of the latter's political inexperience, he soon became not only one of Lenin's earliest followers outside of Russia but also part of his close circle in Switzerland.

It was Lenin who called for and encouraged the creation of an International Relief Organization for twenty million starving Russians, following drought and famine in the Volga area of Russia beginning in early 1921. This was an area that was mostly occupied by the so-called Volga Germans who had lived there since the eighteenth century. As a result of Lenin's encouragement, Muenzenberg founded the Internationale Arbeiter Hilfe (IAH) or International Workers Relief, which became as much an international propaganda as a relief organization. The official founding date was September 12, 1921. International support was recruited for this cause, resulting in large amounts of money being donated from around the world. Many German workers contributed their overtime, often exceeding the eight-hour legal workday to do so.

Loans were floated and farm machinery deployed to the hungry Russians. Later, Japanese earthquake victims in 1923 as well as English striking miners in 1926 also received aid from these funds. Cultural events in the form of concerts, dance recitals, art shows, literary readings, cabaret evenings, and bazaars were organized to support this humanitarian organization, the IAH. Famous German artists such as Otto Dix and George Grosz created art and posters, exhibitions and sales of which helped support the cause.

Martha Scholze, my grandmother, had become secretary of Muenzenberg's publishing company, Neuer Deutscher Verlag (New German Publishing Co.), which he had purchased and that served as the umbrella organization for his future newspaper acquisitions. As he was a sharp critic of capitalism at that time, all his publications combined humanitarian concerns with his strong admiration of the Soviet Union. In addition to her workday, Martha organized cultural and other social events in support of the relief efforts.

My uncle Frank reported to me many years later that after Paul and Martha's marriage, their home was frequently filled with "exciting visitors," members of the intelligentsia, writers, artists, scientists, journalists, and politicians of the same humanitarian persuasion, all supporting the cause. Exhilarating debates were held in the Scholze house, and meals and overnight accommodations were offered. It was a household in "constant chaos." Political affiliation was not the overriding determinant for participation in these events, as both Muenzenberg and Scholze merely sought support for the elimination of poverty through the IAH. Social justice and the alleviation of suffering around the world were the stated goals.

The headquarters of the IAH were located at No. 38 Rosenthaler Strasse in Berlin, which was also the address of the Communist Party Headquarters, where my grandfather was employed as union secretary. At the request of the Party Secretariat, the administrative and powerful arm of the Communist Party Central Committee, he had joined the IAH, was quickly asked to sit on the Executive Council, and soon became one of its most active members. Muenzenberg named himself General Secretary while Paul Scholze became First Secretary. His life now took on a quite different and even more multifaceted role, channeling his influence in directions far afield from organizing and participation in workers' strikes and revolutions. The work in conjunction with the IAH went considerably beyond hunger relief through the organization of food supplies or financial aid. It also established kindergartens, children's homes, orphanages, and schools as well as sending farm equipment to Russia.

In addition to creating the International Workers Relief, Muenzenberg had also become involved in politics, resulting in his election in 1924 as a Communist Party member to the Reichstag, the German Parliament. As a consequence, Paul Scholze, who as First Secretary for the first three years of his membership had in effect led the German section of the International Workers Relief, now additionally took on Muenzenberg's responsibilities by heading the Western European Office from 1924 until 1935. The IAH soon became a worldwide organization. It was referred to as the "third column of Communist politics" and was initially intended to operate only during a particular period of capitalistic society. Its function would be considered superfluous following the presumed victorious revolution of the proletariat. Many countries, including America, India, Japan, Holland, and France had followed Germany's lead and had become members, pledging and, in many cases sending, large amounts of money for Russian aid.

Chapter 37

The Russia Inspection

IN MAY AND June 1922, barely nine months after the founding of IAH, Paul Scholze accompanied Willi Muenzenberg, as well as other inspectors, on an auditing trip of the IAH in Russia. In Moscow they were appalled to discover the lack of control and bookkeeping regarding the donated funds. While workers around the world had been asked to contribute by way of extra labor and large amounts of donated money, Scholze and Muenzenberg, as well as the rest of the inspection team, were met with resistance and revolvers when requesting to see how these monies had been spent by the various agencies. Scholze wrote in a subsequent report that the record keeping of the IAH was in an "outrageous condition and there was no sign of a system in place." A Russian woman employed by one of the IAH enterprises in Moscow confirmed that no bookkeeping system existed within the organization and that this was true of all the IAH organizations throughout Russia!

The delegation found that large sums of money had been misappropriated by private individuals in the most capitalistic of ways. A shoe factory had been created and restaurants and hotels acquired; large tracts of land had been purchased and tractors ordered and received, although the land where some were sent was unfit for growing purposes. Actual financial aid had only begun in 1922, but by July of that year more than ten thousand people had been "employed" at the expense of the IAH in these enterprises. In a publication called "The Third

Column of Communist Politics," Muenzenberg and Scholze sharply rebuked the Russian IAH following the auditors' visit, stating that "never had the International Worker's movement been more cynically abused than through the Foreign Trade Control of the Russian section, that they would lie and seek any means in order to establish private businesses."

In addition to his work with the IAH, in September 1923 Paul Scholze also took on the editorial role of the newspaper *Hammer and Sickle*, German edition, which was renamed *Workers Pictorial Newspaper* in November of 1924. It was a monthly publication, thirty editions of which he was responsible for, and had a circulation of about ten thousand. The last issue under his leadership was published in February 1926. The publication was part of what would become Muenzenberg's propaganda publishing empire and was the most widely read Socialist newspaper in Germany. Most of the photography on its pages was submitted by workers, but by 1927 it also featured photography by the Italian-American photographer, Tina Modotti. In 1925, Modotti, who was at that time living in Mexico with her American lover, the renowned photographer Edward Weston, had herself become a Communist and social activist. The themes of her photographs often reflected the social injustice over land reforms occurring in Mexico. She had joined the IAH of Mexico, and through their respective work they became part of a political community of artists that included Frieda Kahlo and Diego Rivera. As the result of an anticommunist campaign in Mexico, Modotti was exiled and eventually went to Moscow, where she participated in an active political life. Several years later she was permitted to return to Mexico.

In addition to his editorial activities, Paul Scholze was also a coworker and contributor of articles to other journals such as *Der Rote Aufbau* (The Red Structure), a monthly journal devoted to "politics, economy, social politics and the workers movement" that he cofounded with Willi Muenzenberg in 1929. An August 1930 edition featured as its main article "National Socialism or Bolshevism?" written by Muenzenberg. Scholze also wrote articles for *The Red Trade Unionist*, which was published in Switzerland, and assisted with and contributed to the publication of Muenzenberg's book, *Solidarity*, which was published in 1932, shortly after the tenth anniversary of the founding of the IAH. The book tells the short history of the International Workers Relief and would become a classic in the teachings of the early international Communist movement.

A famine of considerable proportions broke out in Germany in 1925, affecting densely populated and industrial areas of Saxony, Thuringia, the Rhine Region, and several other parts of the country. Following so soon after the war years with its deprivations, this was again a catastrophe for workers. The International Committee for Soviet Aid of 1921, whose signatories had included not just my grandfather, Paul Scholze, but also writers such as Anatole France and Upton Sinclair, sent out an appeal to the entire world, asking for help in the same way in which Russia had been assisted following the drought and famine in that country. Their plea included the statement that "the cause of this hunger catastrophe was not, as in 1921 in Russia, a natural one, but rather the result of the bankruptcy of German capitalistic leadership and the breakdown of the German civilian economy." Through this initiative, thousands of children of textile workers, miners, and metalworkers were sent to holiday camps and supplied with food, clothing, and coal. Such aid continued to be distributed to the starving German population throughout the following two to three years.

Turning his attention to a different kind of suffering in other parts of the world in the early twentieth century, Willi Muenzenberg, founder of the IAH, also created the League against Colonialism in 1925 in Berlin. It was, in a sense, the response to mass strikes in Hong Kong, China, then a British colony, and the deadly retaliation by the British, in which many protesters were wounded and massacred. Muenzenberg determined that people who were not yet Communists needed to become politically informed. He was, in fact, considered to be the chief Communist propagandist of the time. Although the stated primary purpose for the creation of this League was to collect aid for China, Muenzenberg proclaimed, "We want to form a holy alliance, we, the white, yellow, black and different colored underdogs ... for the liberation of all those who suffer."[26] There had been many such campaigns throughout the world, and the intent now was to unify them. 'The League against Colonialism' was to be the precursor to the

'League against Imperialism and Colonial Oppression,' which saw its birth at the Egmont Palace in Brussels. This event held February 10–15, 1927, brought together people and organizations, both Communist and those of other political persuasion, who had the common desire to rid their countries of colonialism. The Belgian government had agreed to Brussels as the site, provided that the Belgian Congo and its brutal occupation by the Belgians would not become a central theme of the Congress. Paul Scholze's role at this time was one of "political leader, instructor and advisor," and for several years "Secretary of the Anti-Imperialist League." He was therefore not a participant but rather an organizer of this complex event with worldwide participation.

At the time, Jawaharlal Nehru was probably the best known of the attendees. Thirty-seven countries were represented by 134 organizations, who sent a total of 177 delegates. Mexico sent its ambassador to Belgium. Nehru, a strong nationalist, had become active in the left-wing movement of the Indian government and in the 1920s had called for independence from the British. Upton Sinclair, an American representative, was a writer and a socialist who dealt with social injustice in the many books he wrote, the most notable being *The Jungle*. In it he described the American meat-packing industry and its disregard for basic health standards. Together with several writers of the same era, he was part of a progressive movement calling for reform in society. Albert Einstein, a German-born theoretical physicist and a socialist, participated as one of the American delegates, and Madame Sun Yat-sen, wife of the Chinese political leader who helped establish the Republic of China, represented that country. Nehru, Albert Einstein, and Maxim Gorky, a Russian writer and also a political activist, were elected honorary members.

The 'League against Imperialism and Colonial Oppression' was initially a tremendous success, creating a bond between afflicted nations, but it was not to last. One of the primary reasons was that although the League claimed to be autonomous and independent, in reality it was Communist-administered and financed behind the scenes. Additionally, the Communist participants were not inclined to create alliances with nonrevolutionary organizations. Willi Muenzenberg did not support these extreme, leftist, and exclusionary views but could not control them. They would eventually lead to the defeat of the League's initial goals. Non-Communists either were expelled or resigned, among them Nehru and Einstein, and the League never found popular support. Some of the delegates suffered retaliation on returning to their homelands. Representatives from India were arrested by the British, and the Senegalese representative was imprisoned in France and died there of tuberculosis. One of the representatives to the League from Mexico, a trade unionist, was murdered in Cuba. It was later suggested that Muenzenberg used these events as a front to convert moderates and liberals to the Communist cause.

My grandmother, Martha Scholze, had been entrusted with the task of stenographer for the contributions of the German-speaking delegation. These were later incorporated into Willi Muenzenberg's book, *The Beacon of the Palais Egmont*, the official protocol of the 'League against Imperialism and Colonial Oppression.' A more adventurous undertaking on her part following these events was a voyage to Paris in order to deliver a large sum of American dollars to a participant of the Congress who had been convicted and sentenced to death in absentia in his homeland. Presumably, the money was intended to help him avoid this fate.

When Hitler and his Party of National Socialists (Nazis) came to power in Germany in 1933, the Berlin headquarters of the IAH was forced to cease operation. Muenzenberg withdrew from the organization he had helped found in Germany and moved to Paris. Here he resumed leadership of the IAH World Committee Headquarters and supervised his publishing enterprises. By 1936, he had become disenchanted with Stalin's leadership in Russia and the latter's purges of his opponents. Stalin himself had parted ways with Muenzenberg due to his refusal to "cleanse" the German Communist Party in the same manner and expelled him from the International Communist Party.

Muenzenberg had declined an invitation to Moscow in 1936 perhaps suspecting that he might become a victim of the purges. He remained in Paris, continuing his anti-Stalin as well as antifascist leadership roles, and built a publishing empire that caused him to be later called "the Red millionaire" and an opportunist. When the Nazis advanced in 1940, he fled to the south of France. Here he was arrested and imprisoned in the tiny community of Roybon but managed to escape. Later that same year, hunters discovered Muenzenberg's remains in a forest near the small town of Saint Marcellin, close to Grenoble, showing signs of strangulation. It has never been determined whether he was killed by the Right or the Left, both of whom had reasons to eliminate him.

Chapter 38

Paul Scholze, Politician

IN 1929, WHILE continuing his work for the IAH, Paul Scholze had also been elected to the City Council of Berlin as a representative of the Communist Party. At that time, the Party held twenty-five percent of the total City Council membership. They met in the famous Red City Hall of Berlin Schoeneberg, where my birth was later registered and where decades later the exhibition honoring all the persecuted members of the City Council who had been "kicked out" by the Nazis would be held. As an organization, the City Council had been a potential point of resistance for the Communists against the rise of National Socialists, who up to then had not been represented in that body. This changed in 1929 when thirteen Nazis were elected, with Joseph Goebbels as leader of this right-wing faction. Goebbels would eventually become Minister of Propaganda under Adolf Hitler in 1933. Meanwhile, in conjunction with his continuing IAH responsibilities overseas, Paul Scholze was again arrested in 1929, both in Sweden and Czechoslovakia, and deported back to Germany from both countries.

Following Hitler's assumption of power in 1933, the Communist International, known as the Comintern, determined that my grandfather should be sent overseas in order to "organize international work." The Communist faction within the IAH came to the same conclusion. Looking for scapegoats after the February 1933 burning of the Reichstag, the German Parliament, one month after Hitler became

Chancellor of Germany, the new Nationalist Socialist government planned to arrest Paul Scholze among several other innocent political opponents. However, my grandfather's arrest could not be carried out as he initially went underground. In April 1933, he followed other Hitler opponents into exile, illegally crossing the border into Czechoslovakia, with Prague as the destination. That city had become a haven for political exiles and opponents of the new right wing National Socialist regime. But Scholze remained in Prague only briefly, soon departing for Paris, where he joined Willi Muenzenberg and where he remained with the International Secretariat of the IAH until 1935.

Accompanying him into exile were his wife Martha and son Frank, my uncle, who was not quite five years old at the time. In Paris they sought refuge in the Hotel Bonaparte, located on Rue Bonaparte, No. 61 on the Left Bank of the Seine, in the area known as Saint-Germain-des-Prés. It is even today a quiet street, home to many antique shops as well as the location of the École des Beaux-Arts. The Hotel Bonaparte was a modest hotel, like so many others in Paris, giving shelter to political refugees. There was little money, and Uncle Frank wrote that meals were prepared in the hotel rooms on alcohol stoves. In 1991, while my husband and I were living in France, Uncle Frank came to visit us but preferred to stay at the address of his childhood, the Hotel Bonaparte. He remembered the neighborhood as much as a small child could. As he was a sentimental man, familiar with his father's past, his stay at the hotel and his exploration of this charming and historic area must have evoked many a memory.

My mother, eleven years old at the time, did not accompany her parents into exile. The stories vary as to why this was the case. She was as difficult a child as she later became as an adult, and one theory suggested that my grandparents, in their efforts to escape Berlin unnoticed, feared she might give them away. My uncle wrote that he was taken "because he was the quiet one." It is not certain whether she remained with friends in Berlin or was sent to Sweden to live with an aunt, Martha Scholze's sister, who had married a Swede and had become a well-known author in that country.

In the summer of 1934, Martha and Uncle Frank returned to Berlin. She was convinced that the Hitler scare would soon be over, and Frank, almost six years old, would shortly need to enter school. In order to support herself and her two children, which now again included Helga, my future mother, Martha obtained work in a municipal "Welfare and Youth" office in the district within Berlin where she resided. Each district had such an agency, their purpose being to promote and ensure the well-being of children. Her husband, Paul Scholze, had in prior years been involved in their administration in various districts of Berlin. But for my grandmother, the job did not last long. On January 8, 1936 she was relieved of her duties as a result of her "previously held political beliefs." The letter of her dismissal was signed by the mayor of her district and was to be effective three days later. Martha was now unemployed and impoverished. A political undesirable in a Nazi state, she survived by doing typing work on a small portable typewriter that she still possessed.

My grandfather initially remained in Paris, continuing his involvement with Muenzenberg and the International Secretariat of the IAH, now located there. In April 1935, "with the agreement and joint decision between the representatives of the Central Committee of the IAH and the Central Committee of the Communist Party," my grandfather was sent to Moscow "for further implementation of party work." A fatal mistake!

Chapter 39

Paul Scholze Goes to Russia

FOLLOWING THE BOLSHEVIK Revolution and the abdication of Tsar Nicholas II in February 1917, Vladimir Lenin had returned to Russia from exile in Switzerland and created the Bolshevik Party (later named the Communist Party) and a one-party system of government. A lawyer and a revolutionary, he wished to create a country ruled by its workers and peasants, who would have the right of self-determination and a system of education accessible to all.

Although born into a prosperous family in 1870, Lenin had embraced socialism from an early age. He quickly assumed leadership of the country and remained in that role until his death in 1924. While still at university, he had translated Karl Marx and Friedrich Engel's *Communist Manifesto* into Russian and called for the overthrow of capitalism, which they believed to be an economic system of exploitation of the masses, primarily benefitting the wealthy. In Russia, the tsar and the aristocracy were obvious examples of such a system.

Lenin hoped to create a revolution and bring about a socialist state, believing that his interpretation of Marxism was the sole authentic and orthodox one. As a student, he had studied briefly in Berlin where he had come into contact with Wilhelm Liebknecht, founder of the German SPD party and father of Karl Liebknecht. The latter, together with George Ledebour, socialist politician and journalist, and my grandfather, union activist and shop steward Paul Scholze, had been the three signatories of the January 6, 1919, manifesto declaring the German SPD government under Friedrich Ebert illegal. While Lenin did distribute land to the peasants and nationalized private enterprises, he also created a system of oppression conducted by the state, killing or imprisoning tens of thousands of his opponents, a system that became known as the 'Red Terror.'

It is true that in all political systems there are competing factions and divergent views. This is obviously true of opposing parties but may also prevail within a party whose members nevertheless hold different points of view or wish to attain power for themselves. Certainly, this happened in Germany in the early part of the twentieth century when a split occurred within the SPD party to birth the USPD. Such was also the case in Russia when Lenin, who had been suffering ill health since 1922, died in 1924 following a stroke, which had paralyzed him.

Lenin had long mentored Josef Stalin, a political activist even before the Russian Revolution of 1917, who was now General Secretary of the Party. But his support of Stalin diminished in subsequent years. Numerous protagonists, among them Leon Trotsky, all representing various rival political groups, hoped to become the next leader of Soviet Russia following Lenin's death. It had actually been Lenin's intent to remove Stalin from his position, his assessment of him being that he was too crude, too intolerant and exercising excessive power. In a document which later came to be known as his "Testament," and which was created after one of his strokes, Lenin says of Stalin: "Stalin is too rude, and in this fault, entirely supportable in relations among us Communists, becomes insupportable in the office of General Secretary. Therefore, I propose to the comrades to find a way to remove Stalin from that position and appoint to it another man who in all respects differs from Stalin only in superiority – namely, more patient, more loyal, more polite and more attentive to comrades." [27] But Lenin died before he could accomplish his removal.

Leon Trotsky, who was leader of the Red Army and Commissar for Military and Naval Affairs, was now the most prominent among the potential candidates. He had become a revolutionary, originally opposing Marxism but later embracing it. Like my grandfather, Paul Scholze, he wrote and distributed revolutionary pamphlets, spreading socialist ideas among workers and students, and was several times imprisoned as well as exiled for his political activities.

Stalin despised Trotsky, who was one of the seven members of the Politburo, and considered him to be the main obstacle to his assumption of the position vacated by Lenin's death. Politically split, the Central Committee of the Russian Communist Party, by 1927 headed by Stalin, expelled Trotsky in that year and deported him in 1929, first to Turkey, and later, from there, in 1936 to Norway. Due to Trotsky's continued criticism of Stalin's government while in exile, and his encouragement of mass strikes through his published articles, Norway eventually yielded to Soviet pressure.

Trotsky and his wife were once more expelled in January 1937, this time seeking political asylum in Mexico. Here the internationally well-known artist couple, Frieda Kahlo and her muralist husband, Diego Rivera, offered them refuge at La Casa Azul, "the Blue House." It was the childhood home of Frieda Kahlo and the joint home of the two artists while married. Both Kahlo and Rivera were ardent Marxists and members of the Mexican Communist Party, who believed that political power should reside with the working class. Rivera even depicted his wife in one of his murals in the role of an activist. Because of Trotsky's involvement with the Russian Revolution, both artists admired him, regarded him as a hero, and became Trotskyites.

Not long after Trotsky's arrival in Mexico, Leon and Frieda began a secret love affair, which she validated by presenting Leon with a painting of herself entitled "Between the Curtains." It is dedicated to "Leon Trotsky, with all my love." Initially Frieda's husband, Diego Rivera, apparently encouraged the situation, as it distracted attention from his own affair with Frieda's younger sister Cristina. But the Trotsky-Kahlo relationship was to be short-lived, as Leon's wife gave him an ultimatum, forcing him to make a choice. In any case, Frieda soon tired of the much older man.

As Stalin's power grew among Communists internationally and Trotsky's correspondingly dwindled, Diego Rivera and Frieda Kahlo switched their allegiance and by 1939 had become strong supporters of Josef Stalin. In August of 1940, Trotsky, after several failed attempts on his life, was assassinated, stabbed with an icepick, in Mexico City by an undercover agent of Stalin's. Tina Modotti, the Italian-American photographer and equally ardent Communist and IAH supporter, also shortly died under what were believed to be mysterious circumstances, having suffered heart failure in a taxicab after leaving a dinner party at a friend's home. She had been a member of the artistic group surrounding Diego Rivera and Frieda Kahlo and had returned from Russia, where she had spent part of the exile that had been imposed on her by the Mexican anticommunist government. Later it was claimed she died of natural causes. Nevertheless, the artists Rivera and Kahlo remained strong supporters of Communism and of Josef Stalin. At the time of her death in 1954, Frieda Kahlo's casket was draped with a flag bearing the hammer and sickle, symbolic of her lasting conviction and belief in a Communist system.

Paul Scholze had initially arrived in Moscow in 1935 in order to participate in the seventh and last World Congress of the Communist International (Comintern) held between July 25 and August 20. He was one of 513 delegates who represented sixty-five Comintern parties. Denunciation of fascism was the central theme, the "Resolution" of the event being designated *Peoples' Front against Fascism*. A closing speech given by a Bulgarian Communist politician, Georg Dimitrov, titled "The Present Rulers of the Capitalist Countries are but Temporary, the Real Master of the world is the Proletariat" was received with loud acclaim and long ovation.

It is not known whether it was Paul Scholze's intention to permanently remain in Russia as a result of the National Socialists' rise to power in Germany. It seems unlikely that he would have abandoned his family but rather intended to remain only for "further implementation of party work," as had been agreed to by the Central Committees both of the IAH and of the Communist Party of Germany. Following a thorough review of his own Communist credentials by authorities in Moscow, Scholze became part of a commission responsible for the conversion of members of the German Communist Party to that of the KPdSU(B), the Communist Party of the Soviet Union, the (B) denoting Bolshevik. Many German Communists had by that time emigrated to Russia in order to find work and to escape the increasing power of the Nazis.

But by 1936 Stalin had begun a campaign of repression, resulting in what came to be known as "The Great Purge." Ethnic minorities, wealthy peasants known as kulaks, political opponents within both the Communist Party and the Red Army, religious leaders, and suspect foreigners all became victims of his paranoia and fear of opposition. My grandfather was to be among them. Following dissolution of the IAH in Russia, the NKVD, the Russian Interior Ministry, proceeded to carry out Stalin's orders.

On November 4, 1936, together with six other Communist members of the IAH operating in Moscow, Paul Scholze was arrested and accused of being a member of a "Fascist-Trotskyite" group. It was claimed that Scholze had met with a former member of the Red Front Fighter's League, a German paramilitary organization affiliated with the Communist Party, during his visit to Moscow. The accusations further stated that he had frequent contact with other German immigrants who held "Fascist-Trotskyite" views and were critical of the Russian Communist leadership; that they met in hotels, in restaurants, and in their homes as members of a "counterrevolutionary group."

My grandfather declared his innocence and denied ever having been a member of a counterrevolutionary group or ever having agitated on behalf of one. "During my membership in the Communist Party I was never involved in factions or groups hostile to the Party. I fought with the party against right-wingers and appeasers. Prior to that I participated in the fight against Trotskyites." Nevertheless, he was convicted and sentenced on July 10, 1937, to five years of hard labor in a mine. He was deported from Moscow to one of the many camps known as gulags near Magadan in the Kolyma region of Siberia. It is an area that is frozen several meters deep for most of the year, and the camps were among the most brutal to which Stalin's perceived opponents were sent. While there, on March 26, 1938, my grandfather was again arrested, this time for supposed sabotage, sentenced to death on May 11, and shot on May 22, 1938. As his son, my uncle, wrote to me many years later, it was murder "by his own comrades." He was one of the more than 1.2 million human beings estimated to have been eliminated due to Stalin's Great Purge. Many more died of starvation.

Today a fifteen-meter-high monument called "The Mask of Sorrow" stands on a hill above Magadan, a tribute to the prisoners who slaved and died as victims of the Stalin purges.

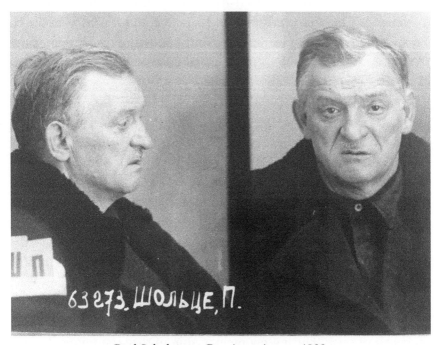

Paul Scholze as a Russian prisoner, 1938

As result of his political persuasions and activities, Paul Scholze had been deprived of his German citizenship in absentia on September 8, 1938, by the National Socialist regime. By then he was of course dead, although as late as 1941 German government authorities were not aware of his murder and still suspected him to be alive and active in Russia. On interrogating my grandmother, Martha Scholze, who was again living in Berlin at that time, as to his whereabouts, their records stated that "in state political and criminal regards, they could report nothing negative about her." She claimed to have had no contact with her husband and to have no knowledge of where he was. In reality, this did not correspond to the truth, as my grandmother had learned in 1938 that her husband had been among the victims of Stalin's Great Purge. In 1945 she remarried, and when she died in 1978, it was as Martha Haeser, with her second husband's surname. Presumably this husband was Jewish, as her remains were interred with his in the cemetery of Weissensee in Berlin, the second largest Jewish cemetery in Europe.

In November 1957, Paul Scholze was secretly rehabilitated as a German citizen, and my grandmother was offered the pension of a "politically persecuted" person. Although living in vastly diminished economic circumstances in the Russian sector of Berlin, Martha Scholze Haeser honorably declined. She had, after all, been of the same political persuasion as her murdered husband.

It was not until October 18, 1991 that Paul Scholze was publicly rehabilitated by the Russian attorney general. On March 18, 1997, my uncle Frank Scholze, son of Paul, was officially notified of this on receipt of a letter from a lieutenant colonel of the Military States' Attorney's office in Moscow. It was almost sixty years after his father's death. On June 30, 1999, the German Embassy in Moscow confirmed this information and sent my uncle the Rehabilitation Confirmation with the note that Paul Scholze's burial site was unknown. No doubt he was among the millions buried in mass graves in Siberia.

My grandfather paid with his life, believing that he had worked to improve the lives of others. At the time of his death, he had lived fifty-six turbulent years.

Part 4

Returning to Happier Times

Chapter 40

More Memories of England

LIFE IN ENGLAND was an especially happy period of my life. On reflection, it appears that my father paid special attention to the daughter he had never really known. He ensured that I now received a great deal of cultural exposure. I relished the attention and the contrast to the small-town life I had lived up to this point.

Knowing of my interest in acting, although not supporting it as a potential career for me, he took me to the theaters of London. One of the most memorable productions we saw was Ingrid Bergman performing in *Joan of Arc at the Stake*, directed by her husband, Roberto Rossellini. The year was 1954. What a thrill to see this actress of international renown in person, not only on the stage but after the performance, exiting via the stage door to enter her car!

Combining my love of English history and the theater, my father and I saw Schiller's historical drama *Maria Stuart*, which depicts the last days of Mary, Queen of Scots. Eva la Gallienne, a British-born American actress, played the role of Elizabeth the First, who caused her cousin, Maria Stuart, a pretender to the throne of England, to be executed. This play was first performed in 1800 in Weimar, Germany, where Schiller lived, and where 55 years later my paternal great-grandfather, Otto Schrader, would be born. Nor did my father forget Shakespeare in this continuing education process, taking me to the original Old Vic theatre in London to see *Macbeth*. Of course, I had to read the text of the play beforehand so that I might understand the language.

Museums also became a new experience for me as I had never been to one. The British Museum was obligatory, although at that age I did not understand the magnificence of its collections and the richness of the many cultures evidenced by them. I could more easily identify with the National Portrait Gallery due to my growing interest in English history. These paintings brought to life its kings, queens, and other notable people about whom I was learning in my new environment.

There was no shortage of castles, palaces, and cathedrals to visit either. Day trips took us to Windsor Castle and its "Great Park," where the spectacular rhododendrons bloomed in abundance in spring. We visited nearby Runnymede, "the birthplace of modern democracy," where the Magna Carta, this ancient document that established the principle that everyone is subject to the law, had been signed in 1215 by King John. Hampton Court, where Henry VIII's trusted advisor Cardinal Wolsey had resided, and Arundel Castle, home of the Dukes of Norfolk, were among other destinations of historic significance. English cathedrals were naturally not forgotten either, most importantly Westminster Abbey, site of all coronations, royal weddings, and burials as well as memorial sites of many of England's most notable citizens. At St. Paul's Cathedral, reconstructed by famed architect Sir Christopher Wrenn following the Great Fire of London in 1665, my father and I climbed to the balcony to hear one another's whispers amplified across the Cathedral's vast dome. Farther afield there was Canterbury Cathedral where Thomas Becket, also known as Saint Thomas of Canterbury and former Archbishop of England, was ordered assassinated in 1170 on behalf of Henry II of England. The Tower of London was an interesting, though grim reminder of all who had fallen out of favor with their various monarchs. Especially moving to a young girl was the story of Anne Boleyn, Henry VIII's second wife, who was accused of adultery and beheaded after only three years of marriage. The most significant mark she left on history was the birth of a daughter who later became the long-reigning Queen Elizabeth I. Each excursion was unconsciously absorbed as a history lesson and breathed life into events of the distant past and the people who had lived them.

Sometimes we took the train to visit the seaside towns of Brighton and Eastbourne with their shingle beaches and, very important to a child, always a treat of long peppermint sticks called "rocks." Brighton was the more interesting of the two; it had a long pier stretching into the sea, as well as the famous and beautiful Royal Pavilion built in the Indian style for George, Prince of Wales, who was later King George IV of England. It was here, far from London, where he enjoyed his liaisons with his mistress, Marie Anne Fitzherbert, whom he wished to marry. He could not do so legally, as she was a Roman Catholic and the law forbade it, but he defied these authorities and married her in secret in 1772. Seen through the eyes of a young girl, whose past had been lived out in the small towns or even villages of Ferchland, Laasphe, and Berleburg, these were all momentous experiences, and their impact has never left me.

For less cultural amusements, my sister and I were taken to Battersea Park, the grand amusement park, which today no longer exists. I don't know who enjoyed the many rides, roller coasters, carousels, and bumper cars more, my father or my sister and I. Going to Battersea meant riding the London bus, naturally on the upper deck, through some of the most industrial sections of London where a strong smell of gas always permeated the air.

Our first real holiday as a family in England took place in 1952, the year after our arrival, when our parents took us to Cornwall, specifically to St. Ives. The destination was reached by train, the nearest train station at the time being in the historic and larger town of pirate fame, Penzance. My father, an avid photographer, recorded the events of this summer, and brilliantly colored and sepia postcards document the scenery. I had never been to the sea, so it was my first exposure to a sandy beach and all that came with it—sandcastles that my father loved to build, seashells, and dead crabs that I studiously avoided. We lived in a boardinghouse near the beach and took the "required" day trips to St. Michael's Mount, the English equivalent of Mont Saint-Michel in Normandy, or the Lizard, the peninsula that constitutes England's most southern point.

Originally a fishing port, St. Ives was at that time already a well-known art colony, where icons of pottery such as Bernard Leach, known as the "Father of British studio pottery," and the modernist sculptress Barbara Hepworth created their work. In the 1970s I returned to this still very small town and acquired several pottery pieces by a student of Bernard Leach, which I treasure to this day. This master potter, who was born in Hong Kong but studied in Japan, "saw pottery as a combination of art, philosophy, design and craft"[28] and inspired in myself the love of ceramics. In his autobiographical book, "A Potter's Book" Bernard Leach states "the essential activity in a factory is the mass-production of the sheer necessities of life and the function of the hand worker on the other hand is more generally human."[29] Not only did I later learn to throw pottery on the wheel, but I have collected ceramic pieces from many cultures. In particular, Native American creations as well as the Mata Ortiz of Northern Mexico have found their place in my collections. St. Ives is now an obligatory destination for art lovers as it has become, since 1993, home to a branch of the Tate Gallery, which here focuses on British artists.

It was in London where I first became what is today known as a "news junkie." My father occasionally took me to Piccadilly Circus in London's West End, where, in the 1950s, there existed a number of underground news theaters featuring the newsreels of the day by J. Arthur Rank, Pathé, and other production companies. Since we had no television at home, these newsreels were no doubt of equal interest to my father. They were always accompanied by cartoons such as Mickey Mouse and Donald Duck or by film clips of The Three Stooges, none of which I ever truly enjoyed. It was the news that fascinated me then as it does today. Piccadilly Circus, with its statue of the winged archer Eros in the center and the flashing lights of advertising billboards, was a wonderful destination in itself. Coming, as I had, from small towns, I had never seen anything like this. Guinness beer and the catchy phrases coined to sell it, using the toucan bird as a mascot, particularly remain in my memory. "How grand to be a Toucan, just think what Toucan do," screamed the text of one flashing billboard. Bovril, Cinzano, and Coca-Cola added their messages. With colors and cars in abundance, I loved the excitement of it all.

The Christmas season meant visiting Harrods, the exclusive department store in Knightsbridge, and Selfridge's in Oxford Street to view their magnificently decorated shop windows. These trips would usually be accompanied by a visit to an ABC Tearoom or Lyons Corner House for tea and cakes. Both had been established in the nineteenth century. Neither chain has survived, both falling victim to a faster pace of life.

June 1953 saw the coronation of Queen Elizabeth II in London. I was already an ardent fan of the royal family, so this was a moment of great excitement for me, as of course it was for the entire country. Since we owned no television, a family in a neighboring apartment invited me to watch the event with them. I was twelve years old and enthralled! I had encountered kings, queens, and princesses only in fairy tales to date. For all the ensuing years in England, I filled scrapbooks with newspaper clippings of the history and activities of the royal family. My father kept every edition of the daily newspapers that featured a photograph of any family member so that I might add it to my collection.

Staff of the German embassy, located in Belgrave Square, as well as their wives, had been invited to observe the coronation carriages' progress from the balcony of the embassy. A photograph of that day shows my father on this balcony, the German flag proudly waving above him, while below one of the carriages passes. Several days later, the new Queen drove in an open car through all the boroughs of London to greet her subjects, and my mother took me to nearby Acton Town where, along with thousands of others, we cheered and waved to her.

In December 1954, just in time for Christmas, an additional sister was born. She was given the names Frances Marion to honor Waltraud's mother Maud who also carried the name Frances. My father was not fond of his new mother-in-law. She had lived a life of privilege, and her sole interests seemed to be attending the opera and playing bridge. During her own marriage there had been household staff, and living without, in addition to being forced to reside in a single rented room in Berleburg after the war, was not to her liking. Her dramatic behavior and self-serving manipulations, which extended to passing food to her natural granddaughter under the table so that I, the child from another marriage, would not observe it, did not please him. Consequently, his youngest daughter would, throughout her life, always be known only as Marion.

In the arena of drama, Marion certainly followed in her grandmother's footsteps. A lively and highly intelligent child, she soon became the center of attention in the family. I was also charmed by this new little being and spent many hours taking care of her, pushing her around in her large navy-blue English pram. While she was still an infant, our parents left the three of us in the care of a relative while they went on holiday. Marion suddenly became extremely ill and had to be hospitalized. It was believed that she was infectious, and she was therefore isolated, visible only through a window for ten long days. While she could be seen, she could not be held. Although my parents quickly returned, they could only witness their one-year-old child screaming behind the glass. This event weighed heavily on them. From that point on, although fully recovered and without any lingering health effects, Marion was coddled even more than before, always regarded as the fragile one and always the center of attention. In her teenage years Marion unfortunately turned to drugs, was treated in numerous clinics in Germany, and was twice imprisoned, once for more than a year as a result of theft in an antique bookshop. Although she married twice and had a son, Marion could never free herself of her addictions. She died a much-too-early death under dreadful circumstances in 2004 at the age of fifty. Her remains were interred with those of our father in a beautiful cemetery in Bonn, Germany.

The happy years in England came to an end all too soon, and once again I was uprooted in the autumn of 1956. Although I kept the mother, this time it meant changing continents. As is typical in the Foreign Service, assignments are limited in duration, and my father's time in London had come to an end. His new tour of duty would take him and his family to America, specifically to the German consulate in Detroit, Michigan. I wept bitterly at once more having to leave friends and, above all, giving up the sense of belonging I had developed at St. Augustine's. I would never again capture it in the American school that followed.

Chapter 41

We Move to America

ON OCTOBER 12, 1956, late in the afternoon, we boarded the Canadian-Pacific ocean liner SS *Empress of France* in Liverpool to occupy our first-class cabins. The ship left the port around 6:30 in the evening, heading for Montreal, Canada. The seas were heavy, and within hours I was, true to form, extremely seasick and remained that way for five of the six days of the crossing. I was confined to my cabin, and the only compensating factor was the handsome steward who waited on me several times daily, usually bringing me fresh fruit. It was only on the final evening, the night before my fifteenth birthday, that I mustered the strength to venture to the first-class dining room. Wearing a green dress that my mother had sewn for me, my face probably matching its color, there was applause as I made my way to the captain's table. A bombe Alaska and a birthday cake had been prepared to celebrate the upcoming event on the following day.

We proceeded through the Saint Lawrence Seaway, the ship allowing a dramatic view of the majestic Hôtel Château Frontenac, which towered above us as we arrived in Montreal, exactly on my fifteenth birthday. From here a Canadian-Pacific overnight train took us, via Toronto, to Detroit. My father documented every step of this voyage with black-and-white photographs, from the moment we boarded the ship until our arrival. And as was his custom, a lengthy trip report later accompanied these photographs for the benefit of family in Germany.

We spent our first three weeks on American soil in an apartment hotel, The Malvern, located just off Woodward Avenue, Detroit's main thoroughfare. It was the time of President Eisenhower's reelection campaign, and we observed his passage down Woodward Avenue in a campaign car, waving to the crowd, while the then currently popular, newly released Guy Mitchell song, "Well, I never felt more like singing the blues," was blasted from loudspeakers mounted on the car. The 1956 presidential campaign was in full swing, and the song mirrored my feelings exactly. No doubt, in those years, a mere eleven years after the end of World War II, it was the dream of many a European to live in America, my father among them. I was merely heartbroken.

In Grosse Pointe, a leafy and wealthy suburb of Detroit, our parents soon found an apartment large enough to accommodate the five members of our family. It was located on the upper floor of a two-story home with a tiny garden in the rear. The owner and landlady lived below. By Grosse Pointe standards, it was exceedingly modest, but for the first time I now had my own room, while my younger sister Gisela shared hers with two-year-old "baby" Marion. There was never a question of buying a house. It was not in my German father's character to owe money to anyone, and no doubt his conservative attitude against such an expenditure had been shaped by years of economic uncertainty. Unlike the American mentality, which would have considered the purchase of a home to be an investment, my father thought of the intended brief duration of his assignment, which was to be only five years.

Grosse Pointe was at that time one of the wealthiest suburbs in America, an island of prosperity abutting the rather unattractive Motor City of Detroit. It was divided into several "communities," each displaying a level of affluence. As such, there was a Grosse Pointe Park, Farms, Woods, and Shores. The most modest, as well as the closest to the boundary between the city of Detroit and Grosse Pointe, was Grosse Pointe Park where our apartment was located.

Grosse Pointe was home to the family of Edsel Ford, son of Henry Ford; the Dodge family, also of automobile fame, resided here. Many of the country's most affluent individuals, though not necessarily the most respectable ones, made their home in Grosse Pointe. The Mafia's Cosa Nostra was well represented by the likes of Pete Licavoli and Jack

Giacalone, both Detroit mobsters, with the latter being implicated in the disappearance of labor leader Jimmy Hoffa in 1982. Some of their children attended the local Grosse Pointe High School, as I soon would. But the 'modest Park' had the advantage of fronting onto the shores of Lake St. Clair with its sandy beach and swimming pool, its lawns and picnic areas, where our family spent many a summer day.

Living in Grosse Pointe exposed me for the first time to the concept of segregation, both racial and religious. Admittedly, I was not aware of this on any conscious level and segregation had not yet become a word in my vocabulary. The world around me was homogeneous, and I accepted this without thought as the norm. In the small commercial area of Grosse Pointe, known as The Village, most of the shops had Jewish names and owners—Stein, Jacobsen, and Himelhoch being examples. The fact that none of them lived in Grosse Pointe but rather at the end of their business day drove to the west side of Detroit was, I believed, merely a personal choice, if I thought about it at all.

At age fifteen, I had not heard of anti-Semitism, did not know that Jews were not allowed to live in the "all white and Christian" Grosse Pointe, and certainly had never heard of a "point system" by which one's eligibility to live anywhere was measured. Private detectives would be hired by real estate agents and a determination of eligibility for purchase made based on "swarthiness of appearance," friends, dress, religion, education, etc.[30] Needless to say, it excluded both Jews and African Americans, although the latter were not designated as such in the 1950s. It was a questionable technique that had been developed by local Realtors to determine whether prospective buyers were qualified and would preserve property values. This system did not see a court challenge until the 1960s, nor legislation to change it until the early 1970s during the Republican administration of Governor George Romney.

The fact that my father did not intend to purchase a home in Grosse Pointe, as he anticipated that his Detroit posting was to be no longer than five years, probably spared him the humiliation of being denied residency. In any case, wherever a member of the consulate lived was considered "territory of that member's country," a consulate being merely an extension of an embassy. In other words, our small apartment was technically German territory. In the event, my father, who loved America, was able to prolong his assignment to almost fifteen years.

Although not a diplomat, my father enjoyed his American assignment at the German consulate. In a letter to his father, he stated that he was not unhappy with his status, as "not being a Diplomat relieves me of many social obligations." As economic secretary, it fell to him to provide the German government, at that time located in the temporary capital city of Bonn, with information pertaining to the political, economic, social, and cultural condition of the Midwestern states that fell into the Consulate's area of responsibility. In Michigan the primary emphasis was naturally on the automobile industry, their manufacturers and the subsidiary companies involved in their production. This provided my father with a great deal of variety, allowing him travel to other states where some of these companies were located. It gave him an entrée to many of the decision makers, both at the industrial, political as well as the important union level in the state of Michigan. Long evenings would subsequently be spent at his desk at home writing detailed reports. He frequently attended the Detroit Press Club where he encountered some of America's great journalists and speakers of that era.

At age fifteen, I was probably one of the least educated young women imaginable. I was now about to be enrolled in the sixth school of my life when I entered the tenth grade at Grosse Pointe High School, and I stood out like the proverbial sore thumb. Coming from a convent school, where a uniform had been de rigueur, I found myself in an environment in which young girls were wearing the latest fashions and looked glamorous compared to my meek appearance. Many had bleached blond hair and wore makeup, cashmere sweaters, tweed skirts, and saddle shoes. I, on the other hand, was only permitted to wear lipstick after my father had checked with a colleague from the consulate whether his same-aged daughter, attending the same school, was allowed to do so. My clothing in no way approximated what the other girls were wearing, but rather what my mother thought appropriate and affordable. Some students had their own automobiles parked in the student parking lot.

All this was bewildering to me. I felt as if I had been dropped onto another planet, and it was not easy to assimilate with its residents. Above all, I had no basis or foundation for the classes that were being taught here. Added to the above major differences between my prior school environment and this new one was my chagrin at receiving my first really bad marks in my English class.

Whereas I had been at the head of my class in this subject in England, Miss Black, the much-disliked English teacher at Grosse Pointe High School, would not or could not take into consideration that I had just arrived from a country where they really *did* know the language, although they spelled certain words differently. In other subjects I not only lagged behind but had never been exposed to them. I found that American history bored me; I had never heard of George Washington or Thomas Jefferson. What was a Constitution, or a mere Civil War when so many more interesting battles had been fought by colorful English kings and queens? Geography, a favorite subject of mine, had been covered in junior high school and was no longer available as a course at the high school level. Greek and Roman history had already been glossed over in a prior semester, and I had to cram the centuries of history of these two important cultures into the few weeks of a summer school semester.

My own salvation in the end became English literature where I did end up in an honors English class with Mr. Schlegelmilch, who became my favorite teacher. And since I harbored vague hopes of becoming an actress, I joined the drama club. Mr. Nelson, the director, soon cast me in another Richard Sheridan play called *The Rivals* and later gave me the starring role in the performance of a Chinese play, *Lady Precious Stream*. This drama was unusual in that it had been written in 1933 in English by a Chinese playwright who was pursuing his studies in London. Although I cannot recall the plot, it is, according to Wikipedia, a "beautiful, romantic drama of love, fidelity, treachery and poetry." I remember uttering the words "filial piety" rather frequently as part of my dialogue. The play had been a huge success on the professional stage and later for amateur groups as well. A photograph of myself in Chinese attire and wearing a very heavy and decorative headdress appeared in large format in the magazine section of the *Detroit News*. I thought I was on my way to achieving the career I really wanted, to be an actress. Surely these were the first steps to stardom!

The Grosse Pointe High School building itself was really quite lovely. Constructed in the colonial revival style with large supporting columns and a tower, it had spacious classrooms, wide corridors with lockers, and a very beautiful library. There was even a cinema where each week a new film was shown during the lunch hour, segmented such that each day one would see a portion of the film at a cost of five cents per day. Today the school is listed on the National Register of Historic Places.

I was no doubt considered an oddity at school as I neither looked nor sounded like the typical American high school student of that era. I made few friends as most of these bonds had already been formed in the younger classes, and I found it difficult to fit in, the contrast from the convent school being too great. Nevertheless, boys began to ask me out, the first one being a certain Vern who at the end of the evening asked whether I would like to go steady. Not knowing what this meant, I replied, "Sure," and was promptly given his heavy silver identification bracelet, so popular in America at the time, to wear "forever." My father, upon seeing this and hearing my explanation the following morning, was appalled, believing I had enslaved myself. This relationship ended with my first teenage heartbreak when Vern decided some time thereafter that he had made a mistake, wanted his bracelet returned, and no longer was interested in me. At a later point he changed his mind, asking me to revive the friendship, but by then I had other male admirers in my life and was happy to tell him so.

These were also the years of my first American social events such as sock hops, junior and senior proms, and Venetian Night at the Detroit Yacht Club, invited by my one remaining friend from my American high school years.

A young man of German descent, with whom I occasionally went out, attended a Lutheran Church in Grosse Pointe Park in anticipation of being confirmed. What this really meant I did not know, but in order to be with him, I too attended and also was confirmed. I had not grown up in a home with religious convictions, my father having officially left the church many years before. He did not condone a state-supported institution, did not believe in a church that by law had the right to 10 percent of one's salary each month, depending on one's declared beliefs, whether Protestant or Catholic. But there was no parental objection to my being confirmed.

Miss Violet Barge at Wynnstay and the nuns at St. Augustine's notwithstanding, I really had no idea what religion was all about. Only much later did I come to realize that in America one's religion and social life are heavily intertwined, that it is important to be not only of the same religion but also of the same branch of a particular faith as friendships are formed and potential life partners considered.

High school graduation approached in the spring of 1959. Although I was not unhappy to see this period of my life come to an end, I had no concept and no one to counsel me as to what I could or should do with the rest of my life. I knew only what I did *not* want. Certainly, I had no ambition to become a teacher or a nurse, the primary professions that seemed to be open to women at the time. I did not know that there were other avenues available to me and therefore could not consider alternatives. At no point had I been given guidance. And if my father had any plans, hopes, or suggestions for my future, other than seeing me married, I was not aware of them. It would not be wrong to state that my parents severely failed me at this point in my life.

I also had no vision or guidance as to how to become the actress I wished to be. Most classmates seemed to continue on to university, with whatever goal in mind I could only guess, and marriage soon followed. It cannot be said that I graduated from high school with great honors. My parents, being either unaware or uninterested as to how to proceed in the American system, only wanted me to be able to earn my own keep by whatever means. The result was a true fiasco. I had applied to and been accepted at a major college, Wayne State University, located in the heart of Detroit, but was obligated by my parents to take courses leading only to another of those most dreaded of careers—a secretary! Surprisingly, they had such a curriculum. In my spare time, I again participated in theater productions at the university theater and appeared in an occasional television broadcast on the university's channel, together with a German professor. One of America's young photographers and artists, named Will McBride, who had been trained by Norman Rockwell, covered me photographically at one of these broadcasting events. The story and photographs with the headlines "Miss Gaby Hesse—TV Student—America ensures its rising TV generation" (translated) appeared in a German television magazine in July of 1960. Will McBride lived most of his professional life until his death in Germany, and while he became extremely famous for his photographic work, his story about me did little to promote my hoped-for life's ambition. Hollywood did not call!

Not long after we had arrived in America, my father became the proud owner of a car, albeit a used one, and the first one in our family. The gray and pink 1956 Dodge, which my father acquired the following year, became the means to live his "American dream" and to see this continent. While our first family trip saw us exploring our home state of Michigan, including the Upper Peninsula in 1957, in May 1959, we also drove to the most southernly point of America, Key West in Florida. My father, always an astute observer and lover of beautiful landscapes, wrote glowing trip reports to his parents of everything that caught his eye. Florida was still considered quite exotic at that time, especially by Europeans. Postwar America, and particularly Florida, was new and shiny and very different from German or English scenery. My father loved the convenience of motels where the car could be parked outside the door of one's room. He enjoyed the lack of formality of American restaurants, the crystal waters and palm trees, and the birds, alligators, and fantastic sunsets we experienced in Florida. I found the landscape flat, unremarkable, and boring.

The faithful Dodge was replaced in 1959 with the newest Chevrolet on the market. It spread its "rear wings" not only in America but also, pridefully, on our three-months home leave to Germany in 1960. Because my father wanted to show it off, but also use it for touring while in Europe, it was decided we would travel by freighter, allowing us to transport the car at the same time. In June 1960, we again made our way to Montreal, this time to board the *Poseidon*, a cargo ship headed to Antwerp in Belgium. Naturally, a voyage by cargo ship takes much longer than an ocean liner, in this instance ten days, as we had to stop in order to unload wheat in Belfast, Ireland. I found it all quite fascinating and mentally incorporated this experience into my growing desire to see the world. No more than twelve passengers were permitted on the ship. This was the limit for freighters, due to the fact that they were not required to have a physician on board. The accommodations were generous, the food excellent, and the sailing smooth.

We made the grand tour of Germany, visiting grandparents, aunts, uncles, and cousins as well as friends in various parts of the country in our huge American car. My father produced the intended effect with his Chevrolet, for wherever we drove, we instantly became the center of attention. An American car of this size and vintage was usually only seen in American films. But the return to the US was inevitable and my future uncertain. With great sadness I said "goodbye" to my relatives. It was to be the last time I would see my paternal grandparents with whom I had lived as a child. My beloved grandmother, Kaethe Hesse, died in 1965, the year in which I gave birth to my daughter, Karen.

Hurricane Donna accompanied the freighter *Transamerica*, which we boarded in Hamburg in September 1960, for our return voyage to Montreal. The usual length of ten days was again anticipated, but after several days at sea we began to experience severe storms and the heavy waves of what was to become the strongest hurricane in the Atlantic Ocean of that season. The captain chose to anchor at sea for thirty hours before entering the St. Lawrence Seaway as it was too dangerous to proceed. Even when he finally continued sailing, the waters were still roiling and tossed the ship from side to side, at times to a thirty-five-degree angle. Furniture was rolling and flying; on one occasion a heavy table hit my mother in the temple and causing a significant cut. Without a doctor on board, the first officer was called upon and very professionally sewed the wound. Even my father's beloved Chevrolet below deck incurred severe damage.

How my report card after my first year at Wayne State University had preceded our arrival in Germany is a mystery to me even now. Strangely, it was lying on the heavy, round oak table in the favored room of my grandparents' apartment, the "gentleman's room." It was no surprise to me that I had failed the secretarial courses my parents had insisted upon, as I simply had not attended classes. While I had done well in others, such as political science, speech, and English literature, the implication of my inability to support myself with this kind of knowledge as opposed to typing and shorthand left my parents quite literally speechless. Not a word was ever spoken about these failures on my part, but a silent agreement was reached between us that my father would no longer pay for my continued education upon our return to America. I was now quite literally on my own, although still living at home.

Unwillingly, against my better judgment and at my own expense, I enrolled in evening courses at the Detroit Business Institute and soon found myself on the very career path I had so determinedly revolted against, the secretarial one. While working part-time in the office of a men's clothing store under the supervision of the wonderful bookkeeper, Mrs. Baron, I attended classes in the evening. But little in my life had occurred without drama of some kind to date, and so it was, that the benign use of a city bus, my only means of transport to the dreaded classes in the center of Detroit, led to another dramatic but this time rather dangerous incident.

It happened on a very cold February night of 1961. The streets were icy and empty when I alighted from the bus on my return home and proceeded down the street on which we lived. My arms were laden with books and a large handbag. I was unaware that another person had followed me on the sidewalk. Suddenly I was grabbed by the throat from behind, a hand covering my mouth. Instinct took over my actions. I dropped books and bag and attempted to free these hands from my throat and mouth while struggling into the center of the icy street, screaming as loud as I could. A young man immediately came running out of a neighboring house, where he was visiting his girlfriend and pushed the aggressor to the ground while his girlfriend comforted me. The obvious intent had been to rape me, as the assailant's clothing was undone.

The police were also there within moments, having heard my screams more than a block away, where they had been patrolling the neighborhood. I was taken to a hospital for examination and questioning. The attempted rape was written about in the Detroit newspapers without mention of my name. Through the articles, which I still possess, I learned that the would-be rapist had recently been released from prison, having served a five-year sentence after raping a twelve-year-old girl. Because no actual rape had occurred in my case, the man was only charged with assault and battery but was convicted and imprisoned for ninety days.

Meanwhile, I continued my secretarial studies. Before long I found employment in the advertising department of *Sports Illustrated* magazine, a division of Time, Inc., which in 1962 also published the still popular *Life* magazine. The limited skills I had acquired in the interim seemed to be sufficient, and I had the good fortune to work for two very gentlemanly advertising account executives in the glamorous Fisher Building in Detroit. It had been designed in the Art Deco style by the famed architectural firm, Albert Kahn Associates. From a gloriously opulent lobby of marble, statues, and gilded ceilings, one of its twenty-one elevators would whip me to the sixteenth floor. Here I shared an office with two considerably older secretaries and fell under the almost fatherly protection of one of my two bosses.

The magazine's head office, with which we had daily contact, was located in New York, and when I expressed a desire to visit and experience the excitement of that city, my concerned boss felt that, at twenty-one, I was too young to be exposed to its temptations alone for an entire week, as had been my plan. Consequently, he made arrangements for me to stay in a hotel suitable for young, single women. He enlisted his friends in the city to ensure that every evening I would be "honorably" accompanied, either to a party or a restaurant, resulting in my first exposure to the glamor of such establishments as the Four Seasons and Trader Vic's restaurant. My days were spent sightseeing alone, visiting the Metropolitan Museum and, naturally, the Museum of Modern Art. China Town, Little Italy, and Ellis Island all became part of my explorations. Although a mere secretary, I was once again beginning to fulfill my yearning to see more of the world.

Chapter 42

I Meet My Future Husband

IT WAS ALSO during this time that through a classmate at the business school I was attending, I was introduced to the man who was to become my husband and the father of my two children, John Lawrence Brooks. John had just completed his university studies, intending eventually to become a history teacher. Following his Reserve Officer Training Corps experience, which had paid for his education, he had made the required commitment of four years of military service in the infantry of the United States Army.

John came from a modest background, although the family claimed descendancy from Henry Clay, an American statesman and US senator from Kentucky in the 1800s. Two of John's three siblings were highly educated, one becoming a vice president of the General Motors Company. The youngest son of the family chose a "life of ease" by impersonating an FBI agent, a federal crime, and as a consequence was convicted and imprisoned.

Soon John asked me to marry him, and together we chose an engagement ring in 1962. While the wedding was planned for early 1963, shortly after our engagement, John's first military assignment as a newly minted second lieutenant required his departure for Schofield Barracks on the island of Oahu in Hawaii.

We had already made many of the plans one makes for an event such as a wedding, when suddenly, or perhaps not so suddenly, I got very cold feet and began to experience strong reservations. Somehow, deep inside I knew, as did my parents, that although John was a wonderful young man, he was not right for me. Only after a number of years had passed, and after it was too late, I understood what my subconscious had been trying to tell me. A paradoxical aspect of his personality, which manifested itself in the aggressiveness required to be an infantry officer, resulted in a certain amount of passivity in his personal life. At the time, prior to becoming engaged, I was too young to recognize this, yet my instinct told me that something was not right. I telephoned John and called the wedding off.

Although I no longer planned to be married, the yearning to see the world remained. By strange coincidence, Hawaii and Switzerland, worlds apart geographically, had long been distant places I had wished to visit. It seemed fortuitous that John was now in Hawaii, and so I planned to travel there in early October 1963, with an option of remaining should I find a job. Before the plane had even landed, I knew that I would stay. The view of the mountain ranges and the blue of the Pacific Ocean were spectacular, unlike anything I had ever seen. The craggy volcanic peaks, the sun, and the palm trees—I was instantly seduced! I had asked John to find me a small apartment for my intended visit, and I immediately set about seeking employment at an advertising agency, the contact for which my Detroit boss had given me—although shortly after hiring me they declared bankruptcy.

I was still there on the day John F. Kennedy was assassinated, on November 22, 1963. A coworker had heard the announcement of this tragic event on his car radio, and as he pulled up to the sidewalk, the staff of the small agency flocked outside to listen to this dreadful news. The shock and grief were enormous. John, who for one month was leading exercises and engaging in war games with a platoon of the 25th Infantry Division on the island of Hawaii, also known as the Big Island, reported that every soldier cried when they heard the news.

My studio apartment on Ala Wai ("waterway") Boulevard in Waikiki allowed me the first sense of absolute freedom I had ever experienced. Never before had I lived alone or had I been solely responsible for my decisions. I knew no one outside of my new work environment. John was housed in bachelor officers' quarters at Schofield Barracks, about forty minutes away, and we saw each other only on weekends. As neighbors I had two homosexual men who, while fighting constantly with one another in verbal battles I could hear through the adjoining wall, were very kind and friendly toward me.

Both rode motor scooters and offered to teach me how to operate one. On a quiet Sunday morning, we drove to a local park where I was instructed. Only one lesson had been omitted, how to apply the brakes. The consequence was that in my desire to stop, I accelerated instead. The choices were few, either dive, scooter and all, into a nearby lagoon or head toward a more solid palm tree. I chose the latter, with more bruising results to myself than to the motor scooter. There were no reproaches on the part of my two friends.

My little domicile was wonderfully placed in that I could walk to all the exciting new surroundings. In one direction, along Kalakaua Avenue, lay Waikiki with all its famous hotels and beaches, the International Market Place, as well as its magnificent view of the extinct volcano, Diamond Head. In the other direction was the beautiful Ala Moana Shopping Center with exotic shops featuring many products from the Orient. Indeed, I loved the whole atmosphere of this island with its mixture of Japanese, Chinese, Filipino, and "haole" inhabitants, the latter being the term for nonnative and Caucasian residents. At the time, only 5 percent of the population was still of pure Hawaiian origin. I did not realize that even here discrimination was practiced in that Japanese inhabitants of the islands, while owners of a number of the large hotels as well as various other businesses on Oahu, were only permitted to live in certain neighborhoods of Honolulu. It appeared to be Grosse Pointe all over again.

Frequently my consciousness is flooded with memories, even as I lie half-asleep, and I could easily transcribe these thoughts to paper. Sometimes I have to dig a little deeper to recall that bittersweet time between being a young, single woman and motherhood. After all, many of these memories have been lying dormant for over fifty years! But try as I might, I cannot dig deep enough to remember why John and I decided to get married after all. I can only surmise that societal pressure or perhaps loneliness played upon me. Most of the young women I knew from my schooldays had married. I had not, and perhaps thought that no one would ever want me. After all, I was already twenty-two years old!

I do recall that when we exited the small church at Schofield Barracks on December 21, 1963, I uttered the words "Oh my God, what have I done?" out loud and silently thought, *I can always get a divorce.* An ominous sign for what was to come. Initially, we seemed to be happy; life had its glamorous moments with receptions and balls, but I found the role of an officer's wife and the expectations stultifying.

Following the bankruptcy of my first employer in Honolulu, I had found another position, again in an advertising agency, thereby avoiding attendance at the eternal "hat and glove" luncheons, teas, and other social events required of the wife of even a low-level officer. We rented an apartment in Honolulu, two residential blocks from the well-known Punahou School, which would later be attended by President Obama. By the time our daughter Karen was born at Tripler Army Hospital in Honolulu in March 1965, we lived a wonderful and casual life in a modest house on the beach in Hale'iwa, on the North Shore of Oahu, just steps from the Pacific Ocean.

I cannot deny that these months were magical. Like my mother, I had not really wanted a child. Having been shuttled around so much in my life, I don't think I knew what the consequences of having one of my own would be. But once she arrived, I adored her.

Our life at the beach, together with our newly acquired puppy Chico, born on the island of Hawaii and transported to us by a friend, seemed pure happiness. John was stationed at Schofield Barracks, relatively centrally located on the island of Oahu and in proximity to Kole-Kole Pass through which the Japanese had flown to attack Pearl Harbor on December 7, 1941. Our occasional visits to Honolulu took us through beautiful vistas of sugar and pineapple fields, always with the mountains as a backdrop. The beach and the warm waters of the Pacific were quite literally at our back door.

There is a saying in the American military population that "if the Army wanted you to have a wife, they would have issued you one," a cynical but apt description of family life in that environment. On Christmas Eve of 1965, John was informed that his unit would leave on January 15, 1966, for a one-year tour of duty in Vietnam, where a bitter war was being fought. It was the army's Christmas gift to us! Our daughter was nine months old. Together with my child and our much-loved dog, I returned to Michigan to be near my parents. Because I had not only a baby but also a pet, finding a place to live with my little entourage was no easy matter. I was not inclined to give up either. My mother encouraged me to inform potential landlords that my husband was an officer, which assumed the respect for such a rank as she knew it from her father's military days in Germany. Her counsel required my reminder that America was in the midst of fighting a very controversial war in Vietnam, and the military, no matter what the rank, was not respected in the least.

Eventually I did locate a rather spacious apartment that met my needs. My divorced landlady was very accommodating and befriended me. Meanwhile I devoted every waking moment of the following year to my little household, having only Sunday lunch with my parents. I walked my baby and dog, sewed clothes, read books, wrote letters and every evening watched the respected journalist and *CBS Evening News* anchor, Walter Cronkite, report on the horrors of Vietnam on television. It was a very long year.

Soon after his return from Vietnam, I noticed distinct changes in John. Already a passive personality, at least with respect to our life together and choices to be made, he became more so. His new assignment, beginning in 1967, was to manage an Army Induction Center in Milwaukee, Wisconsin, which, during those years of anti-Vietnam demonstrations and student riots, was a challenge. I was too young, too naive, and too uninformed to understand why all this was happening and how it affected him. I had no idea of the horrors he personally might have experienced in Vietnam. His almost daily letters to me never spoke of them. Only after his death did my daughter find the Bronze Star he had been awarded for his service there.

Soon our second child was on the way, and suddenly, on January 30, 1968, I became the mother of a son. That year was a politically chaotic one in America, a year of assassinations. In April Martin Luther King, Jr. was the victim, to be followed in June by Robert Kennedy. In tears I called my mother, telling her I was afraid to live in this America. But never could I have imagined that these events were but a preface to the loss of my own, newborn son in a similar manner several years later.

As I stated before, originally, I had not wanted children. Having now given birth to a child of each gender, I hoped my life would be fulfilled, and for some time I did find great joy and satisfaction in this new role. But before long I recognized that motherhood was not enough. There was still a yearning to do something more with my life. I took painting classes, learned to play bridge (badly), and sewed professional-looking clothes. But military life did not allow for constancy, and soon we were moved to Indiana for six months and then to Texas for ten months. John headed to Korea for thirteen more months while I returned to Hawaii with my children. New Jersey followed for a brief time; then, in 1973, began five years in Germany at the European Command Headquarters near Stuttgart.

Neither John nor I had any control over our lives. Initially, the idea of returning to my home country delighted me. It enabled me to be relatively close to my father, who had returned to Germany and to the Foreign Office in Bonn in 1970. It also facilitated my continuing desire to travel. The summer of 1974 saw us heading to Spain. Denmark, France, and England soon followed as destinations. My love affair with France began during this period, and England allowed me to relive childhood memories and renew friendships. We had chosen not to live on the military base but rather to expose our children to the local life and schools. I had accepted a job as bilingual secretary in IBM's laboratory, located not far from our home, which conducted research and experiments in the field of semiconductors. As usual, I wanted at all costs to avoid the role of a typical officer's wife. But our existence had no stability, and my marriage was soon on life support.

Chapter 43

Seventeen Years Later

DURING OUR BRIEF sojourn in Texas, John been promoted to major in the Adjutant General Corps, and it was in that capacity that he had been sent to Germany in 1973. At the end of his five-year tour of duty in Stuttgart, in 1978, he had to return to the US. I had been offered a non-secretarial position over the telephone at an IBM facility near Burlington, Vermont, which I readily accepted. Where exactly Vermont was, I had no idea. From here I filed for divorce, which became final in 1980. After seventeen years of marriage, it was an extremely difficult decision, but it is one I have never regretted. Both children had become fluent in the German language in a very short time and had been totally integrated into the German school system. For five years Germany had been their home, and they were sad to leave their friends when the time came to move back to America. In a sense, I inflicted the same separations on them that I had experienced as a child.

Yet my choice to return to America with my children was based on practicality. I knew that life as a single mother would be very much easier there. In the Germany of the 1970s a working mother was still frowned upon. In addition, the patterns of living in Germany were geared to those of a housewife who could meet her family responsibilities during the day. The shops were closed by the end of my workday, unlike in America, where they were open until late in the evening. Even on Saturdays, commercial life ceased at one o'clock. Weekends in Germany were sacred, intended for family, church attendance or long walks. It would be many years before evening hours or the weekend would be made available for such necessities as shopping for food. Tradition and laws prevented these from becoming part of the German lifestyle. Both employees, and unions strongly fought against it. In 1978 such considerations played strongly into my decision to return to America with my children.

Chapter 44

Life in Vermont

MY FIRST EXPOSURE to the beautiful state of Vermont was an extremely cold one, when I flew to Burlington to find a home for our reduced family unit, my two children and myself. The Green Mountains of that state were completely wrapped in white! It was March 1979; the sidewalks were thick with ice, and the wind, which blew off Lake Champlain, penetrated to the bone, unlike any I had ever experienced. *What have I done?* I thought to myself. But the die had been cast, and although my funds were limited, I purchased a contemporary house situated on two acres of land on the outskirts of Burlington. Its location was somewhat isolated, and whereas in Germany my children had been able to walk to school, they now needed to take a bus.

Both seemed to flourish in spite of their sadness at losing the father out of their lives. We acquired two dogs in addition to the much-loved dwarf rabbit we had brought with us from Germany. This poor, sweet creature was later attacked and killed by a neighbor's dog, causing us all to shed tears. The public schools were excellent, and my daughter, who had always known since childhood what she wanted to do with her life, after completing high school, was easily accepted at the University of Vermont. She subsequently obtained her law degree from American University in Washington, DC. My son, who had declared his homosexuality, floundered for some time, not knowing what direction to take in life. That decision would be made for him by his murder. It was at Karen's graduation from law school in 1991 that I would see Kevin alive for the last time.

The happiest aspect of my years in Vermont was meeting my future husband, Sylvester Miniter, in 1980. A physicist and electrical engineer, he had graduated from the prestigious Massachusetts Institute of Technology, had researched at RCA Laboratories, and now managed groups of scientists involved in designing the logic chips without which none of today's technical devices could function. I have to confess that my original impression of this man was a negative one as I considered his manner to be arrogant. Nevertheless, his insistent pursuit resulted in a slow friendship evolving over the course of a year. Although this relationship developed into something deeper, Syl, who had been raised a Catholic, experienced extreme difficulties extricating himself from his unhappy marriage, requiring counseling to do so.

When we finally married, four years later, we did so twice. The first, a civil ceremony, took place in our home in Vermont in the presence of seventy friends, my sister Gisela, and her young daughter, as well as, joyfully, my two children. A local attorney and a neighbor performed the formalities. Syl and I together had prepared the wedding feast for our guests, he carefully dipping dozens of perfectly formed strawberries into chocolate. It was April, the weather accordingly indecisive and rainy until our special day, when we experienced glorious sunshine. We exchanged our civil vows in our home, decorated with four hundred roses—a wedding gift from a friend.

Three months later, we repeated the ceremony, this time a religious one, in the thirteenth-century Protestant Church in Laasphe, which I had occasionally attended as a child with my grandmother, Kaethe Hesse. The previously mentioned cousin of the blond braids, who had in the intervening years become an interpreter for a German government agency, stood at Syl's side to translate his promises into English. A reception was held in a nearby traditional hotel, familiar to me since my childhood. I did not know at the time that it was exactly in this hotel that the local Nazi women's group had met the night before the so-called Kristallnacht in 1938, when hundreds of synagogues and shops were plundered and burned in Germany, including in Laasphe. Had I known, it would certainly not have been our location of choice for this special event.

All the living relatives, aunts, uncles, and cousins attended our wedding and reception. It would be the last time we would all be together. By the following year, my father was dead.

Before my marriage to Syl, specifically in 1983, I had chosen to become an American citizen on the assumption that I would live the rest of my life in America. I wanted to be able to vote and participate in the American system of democracy. Unfortunately, the German government required that I give up my German citizenship when I made that choice. It is a decision I often regretted in later years. As I stated in my earlier words, I had been lulled into a false sense of security. The country betrayed me when it allowed my son to be murdered, and my sense of belonging has long since disappeared.

My father died the year following my marriage, on October 12, 1985, eight days before he would have reached his seventy-fourth birthday and nine days before my own forty-fourth. His death was not unexpected, as he had been suffering with lung cancer for some time. I had deeply loved him and sobbed bitter tears at his funeral. The ceremony was a civil one, as my father had long before left the church. As previously written, he had never believed in a church supported by the state, as is the case to this day in Germany. His departure from this institution not only consequently relieved him of the automatic tithing from his salary but also prevented any religious observation of his passing.

At the time of my father's death, I had no knowledge of his so very difficult life. Many years would pass before I would have access to the hundreds of documents and letters pertaining to his experiences as a young man. He never spoke of the discrimination he had suffered, of his time in Norway, of the woman he had loved, or of the son, Rolf, he had fathered and left behind. Only a short time before his death did I learn of Rolf's existence.

Chapter 45

I Meet My Brother, Rolf

IT WAS TOTALLY coincidental that one day before I arrived from America to visit my father in the hospital during his illness in 1985, Rolf had called him from Norway. He could not have known that our father was ill and was not even certain that he had the correct telephone number. They had never been in touch. My father had explained to me that his wife, Waltraud, had not wished it. She in turn had told me that the choice to have no contact with his son was his.

It had taken Rolf many years to locate him. His searches by letter had sometimes landed at a wrong address. Even in Bonn, where my father was living, there was a party with the same name as my father's— ironically, an attorney, the profession my father had hoped to pursue. When Rolf heard from my mother that he not only had the correct telephone number, but that I was arriving the following day, he was thrilled and asked that I return his call. In some part of his being, he had always loved the concept of having Gabriele as his sister, which would have been the case had Vivi and Wolfgang been reunited after World War II.

Now we both wanted to get to know each other, but my time in Germany was limited. I suggested to Rolf that we should meet halfway between his home in Norway and Bonn, where I was visiting. My suggestion was the historic and beautiful town of Luebeck in northern Germany. Although I had never been there, I knew it to be the birthplace of one of Germany's best-known authors, Thomas Mann, and that my favorite marzipan originated there. We agreed to meet at the famous Café Niederegger on a Tuesday afternoon at 2:00 p.m.

Syl and I located the café with ease and found it to be extremely crowded. Nevertheless, I immediately recognized my brother in this sea of people. It was as if I were seeing my father as a young man. This was the person Vivi had resented for looking so much like Wolfgang, his father.

We spent three wonderful days with Rolf and his wife, Grete, in Luebeck, this lovely city of the former Hanseatic League, as well as on the nearby beaches of the Baltic Sea. As a welcome gift, Rolf had brought a beautiful oil painting by his grandfather, Vivi's father. This landscape of the Telemark region, where my father's beloved "Rjukan girl" had come from, still adorns our wall.

Rolf's grandfather, a fireman by profession, was also an extremely talented artist whose paintings have been exhibited in the Oslo National Gallery. Rolf also brought with him the photographs of Vivi, both as a young woman as well as in old age, which my father had so angrily swept aside when I had shown them to him while he was in the hospital. For reasons I did not understand, then or now, he had been unhappy that Rolf and I had met. Perhaps it was residual anger at Vivi, who had never come when he had so much wanted her.

Since the day of that first meeting, Rolf and I have been frequently in touch, visiting him and his family in Norway, and spending time together in Portugal as well as in France. On exchanging addresses, we found that we both lived on streets named Red Rock Road, he at number 14, I at number 15; he in Norway, I in Vermont. What were the probabilities of such coincidences?

My father's offspring had now found each other. It was another matter for my mother's three daughters. Several more years would pass before that happened.

Chapter 46

Three Sisters Meet

THE MEETING OF the three sisters finally occurred one year before the fall of the Berlin Wall and sixty years after Paul Scholze's son Frank was born. The occasion, in fact, was Frank's sixtieth birthday in October 1988. Communist Germany had enacted a strange law that prevented their citizens from leaving the country, except for an event ending in a round number, a fiftieth anniversary or a sixtieth birthday of a relative.

My uncle had invited his three nieces to Karlsruhe to help celebrate his special day. Klaudia had applied for a passport six months before, but it was not granted until the evening before her intended departure from Dresden. It was an aspect of the iron control practiced by the Communist regime in order to create uncertainty and affirm dominance over their subjects. She had been allowed to take only fifteen East German marks out of the country for the week of her permitted absence, the equivalent of approximately five dollars. Since East German currency was worthless in the West, she was in effect penniless when she arrived in Karlsruhe. It was a form of punishment for leaving the country, putting her at the mercy of relatives, and it certainly ensured her return. Consequently, we paid for her hotel and meals.

My husband and I had been in Portugal and planned to return to America via Karlsruhe where my uncle lived, and Nicola arrived from England. Although I had met Nicola before, both as a child and later, as an adult, in Vermont, it was the first time the three sisters were together. It was a most unusual feeling, one mother, three daughters, three fathers. But it was not a bond that held. Nicola and I never saw each other again. We lived far apart and had little in common. While we visited Klaudia and her husband a few times in the East, and they in turn came to America, we had no shared experiences on which to draw. The relationships came to an end. We found that having a mother in common was not enough.

Chapter 47

We Move to France

THE FOLLOWING YEAR, 1989, again brought significant change to my life. My husband had accepted a two-year overseas assignment in France for the IBM Corporation. I could not have been more thrilled. While I would temporarily not be able to work, the company generously offered me a leave of absence for that period of time. Only once had I been to Paris, many years before, and immediately had fallen in love with it. I could hardly fathom that now I was to live in this country, though it would not be directly in Paris. Our departure was planned for November, and we waited out the days before our flight in a Vermont hotel room while watching the Berlin Wall being breached and crumbling on television. Although not directly affected by this historic event, I found the moment emotionally powerful. Suddenly it seemed possible that I could revisit the remembered places of my childhood.

Syl's assignment took him to the town of Corbeil-Essonnes, just south of Paris, where IBM had both a laboratory and a manufacturing plant, sister installations to those in Vermont. Finding a place to live was no easy task, though eventually we located a miniature house in the village of Larchant, lying between the pretty towns of Fontainebleau and Nemours, about fifty miles south of Paris. Although the house was of relatively new construction, it was styled as a country home of older vintage, with tiled floors and beamed ceilings. Large French doors opened to the garden, from which we had a view of the ruins of the Basilica of Saint Mathurin, built between the twelfth and sixteenth centuries. It was no longer used for religious purposes, and except for the occasional concert held within the remaining walls, it was now home to hundreds of pigeons. Their cooing is a sound I will always associate with Larchant.

The village we now called our temporary home lay deep in a valley. It drew prospective alpine climbers due to the huge boulders that were part of the local landscape and which presented opportunity to practice this sport without traveling to the Alps. Larchant had few inhabitants, a poor bakery and an even worse restaurant. But both Fontainebleau and Nemours compensated. A wonderful benefit offered by the IBM Corporation, of which we almost immediately took advantage, was a one-month attendance at a French language school in Villefranche-sur-Mer, lying just outside Nice on the Riviera. Beautifully situated, with a view of the Mediterranean Sea, it was also the point of departure for visits to Monte Carlo, Antibes. and the medieval art village of Saint-Paul-de-Vence. Class attendance was quite strict. The day began at 8:00 a.m. when breakfast was served, and until 5:00 p.m. nothing but French was permitted to be spoken. There were no textbooks and no homework. The teaching was strictly oral—from each according to their original abilities to those acquired during this delightful month!

Just ten miles from our little house in Larchant, in the charming town of Fontainebleau, a castle had been built around the year 1137, which during the following centuries was expanded into a magnificent palace to rival Versailles. Among its many occupants had been Marie Antoinette as well as Napoleon Bonaparte. Touring it and the beautiful gardens was obligatory for every visitor to our home. In the early twentieth century, Katherine Mansfield, the well-known New Zealand writer of short stories, to which I had first been exposed in my American high school, had made Fontainebleau her home. She died an early death here of tuberculosis at age thirty-four in 1923. The nearby town of Nemours was less interesting architecturally and was originally primarily a departure point for travel to Paris by train, until I found the courage to do so alone by car. Once I had overcome my fear of French drivers and mastered the Périphérique, the ring road around the city, I did so often. My love of Paris was reaffirmed each time I visited the city, and together Syl and I explored every corner and saw every monument, church, and museum in Paris, while playing host to a number of family members and friends. I still feed on these memories.

Chapter 48

Kiawah Island, South Carolina

AS THE TIME of Syl's assignment was drawing to an end and our return to America became imminent in November of 1991, I frequently had a sense of unease, telling my husband that I felt as if something terrible was going to happen. There was nothing to indicate what that might be, but the feeling persisted even after our return. We both resumed our jobs at IBM. The company had kept my position open, as promised, for the duration of my husband's assignment. A few months later, on April 18, 1992, I received the telephone call with which I began my story. The premonition of "something terrible" had come to pass.

Now was the moment to reshape our lives. We jointly decided to leave our jobs at IBM. The company was reducing personnel and was offering employees limited financial incentives to do so. We took advantage of the offer without any idea as to what to do next. "Where do you want to go?" my husband asked. He would have gone to the moon with me had I wished! Where the idea of Charleston, South Carolina came from I cannot say with certainty, although I vaguely remembered having read about this lovely city in a *Gourmet* magazine article. I had kept the monthly issues for many years, and looking through every back copy, I found the article that had been published in another April fourteen years before.

I knew nothing about the South and had always had a preference for the northeastern part of America. Geographically, culturally, and psychologically, it had reinforced my sense of proximity to Europe and my home country, my own culture. But within three weeks of my son's death, we were searching for a home and quite by accident landed on beautiful and peaceful Kiawah Island in South Carolina.

It could not have been happenstance; it was what my soul needed at the time. The sand and the sea gave me peace and solace, perhaps the same solace my father had always sought by the sea during his own turbulent life. By the extravagant standards of the island, the home we purchased was modest, nestled among palm trees, but it perfectly suited our needs. It was also the only house we looked at before making an instant decision. Syl began a new and very successful career, resurrecting bankrupt companies, while I endlessly walked the beach with my beloved twin cocker spaniels, a gift from my husband several years before. My son had christened them Nicholas and Alexandra, subconsciously honoring my Russian ancestry. We quickly found a circle of friends and our life returned to a semblance of normalcy, with one task, however, still left undone.

Cemeteries are not necessarily tourist destinations but anyone who has ever seen a German cemetery will know that, unlike the majority in America, they are beautifully maintained. Relatives ensure that the tombstones are regularly cleaned, weeds removed, and the flowers kept always fresh. The thought of plastic flowers on my son's grave, as I had seen in local cemeteries, horrified me, and so I searched for sites of beauty where I could bring his remains. Magnolia Cemetery in Charleston was such a place. For hundreds of years, Charleston families had buried their loved ones in this historic site, among the palm trees and adjoining the lagoon with its alligators and the many birds that make it their home. In a plot overlooking the marsh facing the Cooper River, surrounded by live oaks draped with Spanish moss, is where we placed my son's ashes. It was my moment of "temporary" finality, for as my son's tombstone says, "Love is stronger than Death," and my husband and I will eventually join him there.

While Syl was my primary and ever-present emotional support, my daughter Karen had deeply pondered this loss to our family, which was, after all, her loss as well, in the hope of giving my life new direction. While still in law school, she had become aware of the existence of a program within the US Department of State called the International Visitors Program. Its purpose was to invite professionals, who had received particular recognition for their respective achievements in their own country, thereby being brought to the attention of the American ambassador. These individuals, coming from all fields of endeavor, whether academic, political, environmental, or even criminology, were invited to meet with their counterparts in America for an exchange of ideas.

Freelance interpreters were hired to accompany them during a month-long tour that would take them all over the country. An overwhelming majority of the invitees came from the recently reunited Germany, most of them from the East. Their educated citizens would have been taught Russian rather than English as a foreign language and would have difficulty in a professional setting conducted solely in English. My daughter suggested that I was a perfect candidate for such an interpreting position, as German was, after all, my first language. She encouraged me to apply. I was invited to Washington, where I interviewed and was promptly hired. Again, by a most unusual coincidence, the representative of the US State Department who interviewed me and tested my German language skills was herself German-born and had attended language school in Germany together with my "interpreter cousin," the very same who had done the honors at Syl's and my wedding.

The years that followed were to be among the most fascinating and variety-filled of my life. Not only did I travel all over America with these invited guests, but I met people from all walks of life and professions, including the professor previously referred to, who presented me with my great-grandfather's volume on the migration of languages. Depending upon the guest's professional interests, we visited universities and factories, met with representatives in Congress and attended meetings in the State Department. We toured an Indian reservation as well as the site of the Oklahoma bombing, meeting US marshals and local police who had investigated this horrifying event. We visited high security prisons in the state of Washington and Sheriff Joe Arpaio's infamous prison tents in Arizona, where male inmates were forced to wear pink underwear. For several years, I accompanied these visitors, often driving long distances to local appointments that had been arranged by associates of this program in their own communities. At each destination there was usually a "home hospitality" event, exposing the visitor to American family life. These years allowed me to meet people I would never have otherwise met and make friends who persist to this day. Above all, thanks to my daughter, it made for distraction from my most immediate despair.

Sorrow evolves into acceptance as it becomes integrated into one's life. It is not the equivalent of forgetting, as that never occurs. Sometimes fortune intervenes, as it did for my husband and our joint life when he was offered the opportunity of becoming trustee of several companies facing bankruptcy. It was far removed from the technical life he had led and for which he had been educated. But Syl had a brilliant mind, and he immediately became successful, particularly in the financial and legal strategies involved in making these companies profitable again. Above all, he saved many jobs for people who would otherwise have been unemployed, had the companies indeed declared bankruptcy. Additionally, it helped our precarious financial life, both of us having left permanent salaries behind.

Chapter 49

We Return to France

TEN YEARS AFTER my son's murder, the year 2002 became the dawn of a renewed love affair with France. Our chosen holiday destination that year was the beautiful city of Strasbourg in Alsace, the most northeastern region of France. We had found a rental home on the internet and remained there for three months. The area was not new to us, but the duration of our stay permitted exploration of the wider region, as well as frequent crossing of the Rhine River to Germany. Both sides afford lovely scenery. The Alsace, once part of the Holy Roman Empire, had several times in its history changed hands, Germany often being the recipient. It again became French territory with the signing of the Treaty of Versailles following the defeat of Germany at the end of World War I and had once more suffered occupation and annexation by Nazi Germany during World War II. During that period, the population were forced to change their names to their German equivalent, and even streets were renamed to "honor" the Hitler regime. Thousands of Americans had lost their lives by the end of the war in 1945 on the soil of Alsace while fighting for the French in pursuit of regaining liberty for that country.

Strasbourg boasts a magnificent cathedral, many ancient houses, canals, elegant shops, and fine restaurants and was chosen to be the location of the European Parliament and the European Court of Human Rights after World War II. Its glamorous but much smaller geographic opposite, on the German side of the Rhine, is the spa city of Baden-Baden, a favorite of Queen Victoria's as well as Russian writers such as Turgenev, Gogol, and even Tolstoy. They made Baden-Baden their destination in order to "take the waters" at the thermal spas. Since Roman times these waters have bubbled to the surface at sixty-eight degrees Celsius, hot to the touch! Elegant boutiques and restaurants today draw the custom of many Russians and Saudis to the city. A magnificent concert hall, its foyer originally a train station, no doubt drew its inspiration from the Musée d'Orsay's conversion in Paris, which had likewise been a railway station.

Charming villages and vineyards abound on both sides of the Rhine, each country celebrating its festivals, be it the harvest of grapes, plums, and hops, or the local version of Mardi Gras. A favorite aunt as well as cousins lived within driving distance, and we both instantly felt at home in the Alsace. Syl had frequently stated that he felt a greater sense of belonging here than he did in his native Brooklyn, a feeling he ascribed to his maternal grandfather, who had emigrated to America from neighboring Lorraine in the early twentieth century. After this vacation, we vowed to return.

Less than twelve months later, we were the owners of a house near Haguenau, the fourth largest city in Alsace, nineteen miles north of Strasbourg, and had begun its renovation. The section of town where it was located was called Marienthal, "Mary's valley," and was home to both a Carmelite convent and the pilgrimage site of the Basilica of Notre Dame, a convent and center for retreats, run by a small but very business-oriented group of nuns.

It was not the only time that Syl and I bought the first house we looked at, as we had chosen our Kiawah home in the same manner. But this was a different experience altogether! We signed our full price purchase offer, without reflection, for a house we had only seen briefly, on a plain piece of paper on the owner's kitchen table. They were elated, as the house had been on the market for some time. In their words, "The Americans have again come to save us," as they had on June 6, 1944, at the time of the Normandy invasion. But this was June 2, 2003, and shortly afterwards we asked ourselves why and how could we? The interior was hardly inviting. Although all doors and windows opened onto several terraces, the house itself was dark, with horrendous wallpaper covering even the ceilings. The rooms were small and made more so by heavy, dark furniture. A huge stone fireplace, fit for a traditional French farmhouse, took up almost an entire wall in the small living room. It required imagination to consider living here. But the land was generous, and the possibilities we visualized, including a swimming pool in place of the potatoes currently planted, were carefully and perfectly carried out by the wonderful Polish architect we found, just by chance, in the nearby city of Haguenau.

My own dream of a home in France had been a far cry from what we had now acquired. No doubt influenced by the charming Peter Mayle book, *A Year in Provence*, I had envisioned a similar experience in a tiny village where we would do our shopping in a nearby *boulangerie* (bakery) or marketplace, where we would meet our prospective new neighbors in cafés every day. But Syl was of another opinion, and he prevailed. He was still actively involved with running the companies he had rescued, and he needed to be near an airport for frequent return trips to America. I added the hoped-for "Provence" feeling to our new property by planting ten cypress trees, which grew to a substantial height, and installed an impressive wrought iron gate.

In the tiny village of my imagination, I had wanted a small house surrounded by a high wall that would shelter a garden, alive with many flowers. Instead, we had acquired a large piece of property, and the wall was limited in height due to specifications imposed by the town of Haguenau. Nor was there a market in our village, and the products of the only boulangerie were not to our liking. The biweekly market was held in Haguenau's market hall, the Halle aux Houblon, the Hops Hall, where every August the colorful Hops Festival was celebrated. It was located several miles away in the center of the city but had none of the romance I had hoped for while shopping for food in France. Instead, the necessity for provisions led to a weekly outing to the German side of the Rhine, to a local supermarket, and was always accompanied by a delightful lunch with my husband.

By 2003, the world was firmly ensconced in the digital age, and Syl had encouraged me to turn my continuing photographic interests toward a digital camera. It was a daunting prospect, as I was not in the least technically talented or inclined. While still living in America, I had purchased a small model of such a camera and taken a brief workshop in Delray Beach, Florida. The results were encouraging, and once I became settled in France, I was asked to exhibit my photos in independent shows, both in Strasbourg as well as in locations closer to home, near Haguenau. Some were hung in a restaurant, and several of my images appeared in the *Dernières Nouvelles d'Alsace*, the regional newspaper.

Shortly after moving to our new home, I joined a local photography club, a large group of hobbyists who met every two weeks. Although I considered myself technically weak in the art, I knew that I had a good eye, and there is no doubt that my photographs were the equal of most of the members' achievements. I became active in photographing local festivals, and my efforts were represented in their annual group shows.

On three occasions, I participated in photo workshops with a professional photographer, flying back to the United States to do so. One of these workshops took me along America's famed Route 66, another to Monument Valley and the surrounding spectacular areas of Utah, as well as a later one to the beautiful mountains of Colorado. In France, along with a very small group of international photographers, I took part in a workshop in the Department of the Lot in southern France, where we were housed in a small chateau. My camera never left my side as we continued our travels throughout Europe as well as to other continents.

It is easy to be charmed by a country that exudes history, obliging one to reflect on the fact that people have lived, loved, and toiled here for centuries, in many cases in the very buildings still standing and occupied today, where there is evidence of earlier habitation by ancient civilizations in both the architecture and the remaining ruins. Enticing books are published about the prettiest French villages, and we did our very best to visit as many regions of this lovely country as we possibly could.

Strasbourg calls itself "The Crossroads of Europe" as indeed it lies in its very heart. It was an easy point of departure for other destinations—the Tyrol in northern Italy, Sicily, Venice, Morocco, Tunisia, Norway, Greece, Poland, the Czech Republic, and Russia, to name just a few.

Even Egypt was accessible by a single flight. We cruised the Nile River and Lake Nasser, toured Cairo and Alexandria, visited mosques, museums, and the great Pyramids. The memories are not just etched in our hearts but documented by thousands of my photographs. My desire to see the world was well gratified during these years.

But what is a country without people, without friends? Those were sorely lacking in our new environment. It is not a condemnation of the French to state that we made very few friends while living where we did. Rather, it is an acknowledgement that the Alsatian character is unique, shaped no doubt by its turbulent history. Ever since Julius Caesar captured the area at the battle of the Vosges in 58 BC against Germanic tribes, it was tossed back and forth between the Alemanni and the Franks. At times, it was French, and at the end of the Franco-Prussian War, in 1871, it became German, being under the sole authority of the German emperor, Wilhelm II. Although the Treaty of Versailles, following German defeat at the end of World War I, returned Alsace to France, it was again occupied and annexed by Germany during the Nazi Years of 1940–1945.

Alsace has at various times been predominantly Protestant, at other times Catholic. Jews were always a minority population and historically were segregated, primarily allowed to live in villages as opposed to the cities. It is perhaps not surprising that the people turned inward, protective of their own ways and culture. Unlike America, where almost all citizens have roots in a place other than where they are currently residing, the opposite is true in the Alsace. The majority of the population not only came from their immediate surroundings but received their education and subsequent employment there. Their friendships were formed in their early years, and now they raise their own families in the same environment. They have no need of outsiders, not even of French citizens from other regions of the country, who often find it equally difficult to form friendships. Only in the younger generation did we notice a distinct difference. The highly educated children of my generation have frequently chosen to live and work elsewhere and, not infrequently, abroad.

Language was of course an obstacle. Although I spoke both French and German, Syl spoke neither. German, the language of the former occupiers of Alsace, and the local dialect that had evolved from both languages and that Alsace was desperately trying to preserve, were widely used. But our inability to communicate as a couple was an impediment. We had wonderful neighbors, very few close friends, and some casual acquaintances, but frequently I was alone, as Syl had to return to America for business reasons. I suffered for the lack of more companionship in my life.

It was with a heavy heart that I decided in 2013 that my love affair with France had come to an end after ten years. We had never become integrated, and while this did not disturb Syl, who was kept occupied telephonically with business affairs in America on a daily basis, for me life became lonely. While still residing there, I casually began a search on the internet for a house in a neighborhood with which we were familiar in America. Serendipity led me to a home reminiscent of our house in France and Syl asked whether I would be willing to fly to this location to look at it.

I arrived on a Saturday, and as was our custom, on Monday I purchased the house. We prepared our belongings in France and shipped them across the Atlantic while waiting for a buyer of our home in Alsace, which Syl had never really wanted to leave. It did not matter to him that we knew few people, but he understood my loneliness and agreed to return to America.

But the time was not right. No one wanted this lovely house and garden, this special environment we had created in Marienthal. The furniture was now gone, sent to the newly acquired home in the United States, giving us little option except to keep the property in Alsace. We decided to divide our life between the two countries for the foreseeable future. After we established ourselves in America, I flew back to France to refurnish our empty home, and we continued to use it as a base for our travels. Six years later, in 2019, when the house was again on the market, we signed the documents of sale with the first family to view it, who immediately fell in love with it. Our home and friends in America welcomed us back.

Part 5

Turning Back the Clock

Chapter 50

The Extended Family

THROUGHOUT THE DOCUMENTED centuries of my Prussian ancestors' turbulent lives, there are those who chose to make contributions to society through more peaceful and creative accomplishments. My great-grandfather Moritz did so as a judge and author of law books. His son, my grandfather Walther, likewise chose the legal profession, and his sister, my great-aunt Alice, became a teacher. Unusual for the times, their parents—Moritz, the converted Jew, and his Christian wife, Maria Pesch—had encouraged their daughter to become as educated as possible. While Alice did not remain a teacher in the precise definition of that word, she, together with her future husbands, left a lasting impact on our everyday lives.

In an elegant section of Munich in Bavaria, there is a cemetery reserved for the privileged and the prominent. Included in this prerequisite for burial are artists, scientists, politicians, and civil servants, among many other well-known personalities who, in their lifetime, made a special contribution to the city of Munich. Among this list of notables is my great-aunt Alice, Freifrau von Pechmann, born in 1882, one year after her brother, my grandfather Walther Hesse. The title *Freifrau* is the equivalent of *baroness* in the English titled world. Alice's remains are interred with those of her second husband, Baron Guenther von Pechmann, as well as with those of his parents and a number of close relatives of their family.

It is assumed that the cemetery dates to the ninth century, probably serving as the final resting place for the inhabitants of what was then a village called Bogenhausen. Not until the nineteenth century did it become a part of Munich. Generally, cemetery plots here are reassigned after fifteen years, although for the most prominent the tombstones remain. The Empress Soraya, second wife of the Shah of Iran, formerly Persia, whose mother was German, rests here, as does her tombstone. The internationally known film director and playwright Rainer Werner Fassbinder, and one of Germany's best-known writers, Erich Kaestner, are further examples. Kaestner, a German author, poet, satirist and prolific journalist, is perhaps best known for his beloved children's books including *Das doppelte Lottchen*, later made into the American film *The Parent Trap*. The German version, created in 1950, was the very first film I saw as a child. My uncle, Frank Scholze, had appeared in both a film and a stage version of Kaestner's book *Emil and the Detectives*, which has been translated into fifty-nine languages.

Great-Aunt Alice and her second husband are among those whose tombstones remain, today even pictured on a Wikipedia website, as both were significant contributors to the culture of their time. But Alice had a life before she became the wife of a baron. As a young schoolteacher, at age twenty-three, she had married Werner Hegemann in 1905. Born in 1881, the son of a manufacturer, Hegemann had studied history and economics at universities in Berlin and Strasbourg, followed by Munich, where they apparently met. Supported and encouraged by her family, Alice subsequently also enrolled to study economics in Munich. By 1906, their daughter Ellis was born, and in 1908, the family traveled to the United States with their two-year old child.

Chapter 51

Werner Hegemann, City Planner

HEGEMANN WAS IMPRESSED by the advocacy for social reform he encountered in America, particularly in connection with architecture and urban housing projects. In Philadelphia he visited various exhibitions by the newly created Housing Inspection, as well as the Committee on Congestion in New York. It was during this time in America and the projects to which he was exposed there, that Hegemann conceived the idea and became the organizer of an international competition for an overall development plan for the city of Berlin. He proposed that this competition should be held in that city, and at only twenty-eight years of age, Hegemann was named the General Secretary of the International City Planning Exhibition. In 1910, the results of this competition were exhibited and subsequently made public in other German cities, as well as being shown in London. As a consequence, Hegemann traveled widely and was frequently absent. He appeared as a speaker on not only city planning but also politics, as he had meanwhile become a member of the left-leaning Socialist Party. He wrote prolifically, and in 1911 as well as in 1913, he published the two volumes that served as foundational documents for this new discipline called city planning.

Alice, although educated as a teacher, shared her husband's interests and wished to contribute her own ideas and critiques regarding his projects. It seems that this was not something her husband's ego could accept. She had not studied in the same fields as he, had not actually received a university degree, and certainly had not earned a doctorate as he had. All these factors probably contributed to his dismissal of her thoughts and talents. Alice felt underestimated and excluded from his work. Their marriage had already suffered due to his frequent absences, so that when he returned to America in 1913 and continued his career, he did so alone.

In Boston, Werner Hegemann became a member of the Exhibition Committee for Boston 1915, a philanthropic project to make Boston a model city. He had been invited by the People's Institute of New York to lecture in America about city planning and did so in more than twenty cities. At the beginning of World War I in 1914, the final cities on his lecturing itinerary were Oakland and Berkeley in California. Planning to return to Germany, he chose the Pacific route home to Europe. However, his ship was seized by the British off the coast of Africa and the passengers interned in Mozambique. Posing as a blind man, he managed to escape and stow away on a Norwegian vessel that was headed back to America, taking him to a southern port. From there he returned to New York, where he remained until well after the end of World War I.

In 1920 he met and married the daughter of an immigrant German physics professor at the University of Michigan in Ann Arbor. With her, he eventually returned to Europe and, after an extended stay in Naples, Italy, returned to Germany. With his new wife Hegemann had four more children. Back in Berlin, he edited a magazine that covered international architecture together with his own critiques. He lectured on what he called "moderate modernity" in architecture and wrote several books, the best known-of which is called *Stony Berlin: History of the Largest Tenement City in the World.*

Hegemann's political writings frequently turned to warnings about the rise of the National Socialists, culminating in a book called *History Unmasked*, which he cynically dedicated to Adolf Hitler. When Hitler came to power in March 1933, Hegemann was denounced as a "historical forger."[31] His books were considered subversive and were included in the great book-burning campaigns conducted by the German Student Union in an "action against the un-German spirit," a literal cleansing by fire of hundreds of Germany's literary contributions.

Shortly after this event, Hegemann fled Germany with his new family by way of Switzerland and France and returned to America, where he had been invited to teach at the New School of Social Research in New York. The Nazis had meanwhile confiscated the home he had designed and built for his family in Berlin and revoked his doctorate. In 1934 Hegemann had critically written that the "persecution of Jews in Germany was in conformity with the old Prussian tradition of antisemitism and was consistent with the German aristocracy's lack of interest in intellect and higher culture."[32] This must have been perceived as an insult to former friends within the aristocracy, such as Guenther von Pechmann. Nor could such commentary have endeared him to the new government of Germany. Hegemann never returned to his home country and died in New York of complications from pneumonia in 1936 at the age of fifty-five.

The city of Bonn, which functioned as Germany's capital after World War II and for a number of years after reunification in 1989, is also a university town and boasts a beautiful baroque city hall on its marketplace. On May 10, 1933, a very large book burning was carried out on this square. Today it is a bustling place with restaurants, cafés, and a busy market atmosphere. Easily missed are the bronze memorial and the fifty bronze "bookmarks" scattered among the cobblestones, which I noticed quite by accident in the summer of 2019. Each bears the name of a well-known writer considered during the Hitler years to have been subversive. Among them is the name of Werner Hegemann, my great-aunt's first husband and briefly my relative by marriage, as well as Erich Kaestner, mentioned earlier. Although not Jewish, Kaestner was a pacifist and had been critical of the Nazi regime, making him and his books equal targets for burning.

Chapter 52

Baron Guenther von Pechmann

AMONG HEGEMANN'S CIRCLE of good friends was Baron Guenther von Pechmann, whose interests were closely aligned with Hegemann's. He had introduced his wife Alice, my great-aunt, to von Pechmann, who subsequently became her friend and confidante. While von Pechmann was not himself concerned solely with architecture or public housing, he was an early adherent of the movement known as *Deutscher Werkbund* or German Federation. This was an association of craftsmen, formed in 1907, which consisted of architects, artists, and designers whose primary goal was to integrate art and crafts with industrial mass production. By the beginning of World War I, the movement had almost two thousand members in six countries.

This movement differed from the Arts and Crafts movement, which had seen its birth in Britain in the 1860s, in that the Werkbund did not reject, but rather promoted machine-made products. However, the Arts and Crafts credo of "form follows function," thereby eliminating excessive decoration, was also subscribed to by this German association. The concept created not only efficiencies in manufacturing, but also quality in design, making products available to all levels of society, be it in architecture or common household goods.

It was as much an economic movement as it was an artistic one, and it greatly enhanced Germany's foreign trade and competitiveness, largely through the emphasis on quality. The German Federation was, in a sense, the precursor of the Bauhaus school of design, founded by the architect Walter Gropius in 1919 in Weimar, birth city of my paternal great-grandfather, Otto Schrader. Coincidentally, 1919 was also the year of his death.

The "friend and confidant" relationship between Alice Hegemann and Guenther von Pechmann developed into a love affair. In 1918, she married into an aristocracy that dates back to 1697 and was easily integrated into a warm and caring family. Their first child, a son whom they called Eckehart, was born in 1920, followed by a daughter named Sibylle in 1922.

Guenther von Pechmann was born in 1882, the same year as Alice, in Neu Ulm, Bavaria. Initially, he chose to become a career officer in the military but by 1903 had decided to study both law and economics. He attended universities in Munich and Freiburg in the Black Forest, although he was retained as a reserve officer of his regiment. Having completed his studies, von Pechmann was asked to oversee the preparations for the Exhibition Munich 1908, and for the following five years he headed a state office whose purpose it was to coordinate and support the implementation of the applied arts commercially. In industry this meant the creation of aesthetically appealing everyday objects in the manner of the German Federation, which he had joined in 1910.

When World War I broke out in 1914, von Pechmann immediately rejoined the military. In 1916, he was awarded the highest honor given by the kingdom of Bavaria for bravery, the Military Order of Max Joseph, which had been founded by the first king of Bavaria in 1806. Had he not already been a member of the nobility, this award would have bestowed that honor on him, although the title received in this manner would not have been hereditary. Since at the end of the war the monarchy of Bavaria collapsed, making the order obsolete, this was of no consequence to von Pechmann. He continued his doctoral studies, completed his dissertation, and entered the world of industry for some years.

In 1925 Guenther von Pechmann was entrusted with a newly established department for commercial art in the Bavarian National Museum in Munich, one of the largest art museums in Germany. Under his leadership, the department created the first European collection of "modern commercial art," with examples dating back to 1840.

But von Pechmann's interests extended beyond the arena of art collections and included guidance for the curricula of trade and public schools on such subjects as art appreciation and the formation of tasteful design in a younger generation.

By 1929, Guenther von Pechmann had been named director of the State Porcelain Manufactory, formerly the Royal Porcelain Manufactory, as it had been founded in 1763 by King Frederick II in Berlin. With the implementation of "simplicity in design," von Pechmann was able to manufacture quality porcelain for everyday use, making it available to all classes rather than only the wealthy, while at the same time achieving financial health for a company that had been struggling through the economic crisis gripping the world.

Graver times were to come when Adolf Hitler was elected Chancellor in 1933 and the National Socialist Party began to control German society. Guenther von Pechmann refused to join the Party on principle, and Alice was no longer allowed to work, as she was half-Jewish, suffering a similar fate as had her brother Walther and my father, Wolfgang, her nephew. In 1938, Guenther von Pechmann was pressured and finally dismissed from his position as director of the State Porcelain Manufactory, with the baseless accusation of bad management. He and his wife lived out the remainder of the war on a family estate near Lake Constance. Alice later spoke of having hidden a number of valuables on the grounds of the large estate during the war but unfortunately could not remember where. In 1946, the year following the war's end, Guenther von Pechmann returned to his earlier position at the Bavarian National Museum, and in 1962 the German government honored him with the award of the Order of Merit of the Federal Republic of Germany, which is granted for achievements "that served the rebuilding of the country in the fields of political, socio-economic and intellectual activity, and is intended to be an award of all those whose work contributes to the peaceful rise of the Federal Republic of Germany." [33]

Chapter 53

Baroness Alice von Pechmann, Great-Aunt

ALICE HEGEMANN, MY grandfather Walther Hesse's sister, could not have found a better partner in life than Guenther von Pechmann. It must have been a moment of great joy when she entered into marriage with a man, whose artistic and commercial activities coincided with her own interests, who welcomed her contributions and made no attempt to stifle her ideas. I do not know whether it was her innate talent and taste or whether she had indeed studied design and interior decorating, but she applied her creativity in both fields in the years to come. One of her contributions in the arena of design was lamps and particularly lampstands in porcelain, examples of which can still be found among items auctioned on the internet. Her influence on the simplicity of porcelain design, implemented by the company her husband was directing, can be seen in a cup and saucer she created in 1930, which was included in a Museum of Modern Art exhibition in New York.

Alice von Pechmann, great-aunt

Late in the nineteenth century, an art magazine named *Der Kunstwart* (*The Art Warden*) had been established and published, first in Dresden and later in Munich. It was a publication geared to the cultural education of the younger generation and dealt with a broad spectrum of subjects falling under the classification of contemporary arts. A monthly journal, it focused on "all things beautiful" relating to "art, literature and life." As such, it included poetry and articles on theater, music, and the applied arts. My great-aunt Alice became a contributor to *The Art Warden*, writing an essay in the January 1929 edition that concerned itself with the design of furniture being created by *Deutsche Werkstaetten* (German workshops) located in Dresden.

Both Alice and her husband were promoters of simplicity, functionality, and availability of beautiful things to all classes of society. In that capacity, they were supporters of the manufacture of modular, prefabricated furniture, shipped in sections and assembled in place, which afforded the possibility of such a lifestyle. They were created by these workshops and designed to modernize the German home. In her essay, Alice praises the fact that since the first modular furniture appeared in 1908, the company had always kept in mind artistic design and economic use of materials to make furniture affordable to a wide segment of the general public. She suggested that one's living space should be considered an "organism" that, in conjunction with this new style of furniture, could be created by the selection of "fabric, carpets, wallpaper, glass and even metal items" to form a whole of "light, clarity, love of color"—in other words, an "affirmation of life." This movement toward simplicity was in direct opposition to that of Art Nouveau, with its emphasis on intricate and floral design, which was popular in Europe at the time.

Although Alice had married into the aristocracy, it is remarkable how her writings concern themselves with the well-being of the socially less privileged. This is particularly expressed in a lengthy article she wrote for *The Art Warden* concerning the influence of women on their surroundings. While she recognizes that the affluent can have direct involvement in the creation of their prospective home in consultation with an architect, during Alice's lifetime this was becoming less and less the case. Capitalist investors were now dominating the building market and creating apartments for the masses. There was no opportunity to accommodate to individual tastes or wishes. No doubt, her father, my great-grandfather Moritz Hesse, had some influence on her thinking during her formative years, as Moritz had socialist leanings throughout his life and contacts with prominent socialists during his later years. Additionally, the concern of Alice's former husband, Werner Hegemann, for public housing for the less affluent classes of society, which he had learned about in America, must have left an impression on Alice. In her article, Alice references the American method of "series building," the "typifying" of houses at "astonishingly low prices," allowing people of all economic levels to acquire their own homes. She advocates the sense of space created in such houses and the integration of various functions into those spaces, positively contrasting this building method to the small, often dark individual rooms in German apartments of that era. She again emphasizes sparseness in the number of objects with which one should surround oneself and notes that simplicity, the sense that "less is more," is important, that the "freeing oneself of life's 'ballast' should be the First Commandment."

In addition to her published articles, Alice von Pechmann in 1929 also compiled a book of essays simply entitled *German Workshops* in recognition of the thirty years of existence of this enterprise. Complete with photos typifying this school of design, whether furniture, fabric prints, or glassware, the essays were contributed by well-known contemporaries, the tastemakers and shapers, among them composers, writers, and artists. Commercial art was also given its rightful place in this publication, as the journal is complete with advertising for fashions, cars, and even moving companies. Alice gave due credit to all forms of art with this commemorative work. I was fortunate to find the one existing copy in America in a specialty bookshop in Pennsylvania.

Guenther and Alice von Pechmann had both lived full and creative lives. He died in 1968 and she in 1976. Both had served their country in extraordinary and measurable ways, socially, economically, and artistically. The creative vein continued to run strongly through the family. Their daughter, Sibylle, became a talented painter, while their son Eckehart's daughter, Gabriele von Pechmann, (with whom I share a first name), chose to become a goldsmith. Gabriele, her sister Beatrix, and I have recently found each other. While this family line has been immortalized in a recent German novel, it is my personal contact with my 'newly-found' second cousins that brings my own family chronicle to a close.

Epilogue

Writing about one's family can be a perilous journey. There are no maps telling one where to go or how to get there, only words relating where others have been. History has idolized some members and condemned others, each according to the times in which they lived and the roles they played. Personally, I have known relatively few members of my large family and learned of the intimacy of their lives through letters, written either by or to them. They all remain in my possession.

My father created a brief summary of his immediate forebears and sent me copies of his uncle's attestations to being born "Aryan"; however, he died before he could continue to document his family more completely. The archives of Riga in Latvia were helpful in that regard, providing me with information pertaining to my paternal great-great-grandfather, Jacob Heinrich von Wilm, and his descendants. I have created family trees with information derived from both these archives and ancestral websites, including one specifically dedicated to Jewish genealogy in Germany. The latter was helpful in the identification and verification of my Jewish great-great-grandfather Moritz's family, as well as of subsequent generations on my father's side. And scouring the depths of the internet over many years has helped in locating additional relatives.

Documentation of the Hesse family's difficulties as a result of their Jewish ancestry is in my files, as are my father's many letters to his "beloved Vivi" and his correspondence with his own father.

Letters from my birth mother, Helga, sent to various friends and relatives, as well as to my half-sister Klaudia, are also in my possession and have been preserved in a thick binder. They adequately convey her personality.

The uncle I did not meet until I was in my forties, Helga's brother, supplied me with virtually hundreds of personal letters, published documents, books, and photographs pertaining to his own father's and my maternal grandfather's life. They have been the source for most of the information I have used in my writing. Quotations without an identified source are taken from my personal records. History books, biographies, and countless articles in the public domain have also been of great help and are appropriately referenced.

It was not my intent to rewrite the history of Germany or the two World Wars. Historical events occurring throughout those years are only described to the degree they affected and helped shape the lives of my family, including myself. I apologize in advance for any possible historical inaccuracies.

Needless to say, descriptions of my childhood are almost entirely based on memory, with the exception of quotations from family letters that described my circumstances. Over the years I have kept journals in which I frequently recorded information imparted to me by members of my family. I have drawn on these to complete prior knowledge I might have had of an individual. The interesting but often difficult circumstances of my family's lives have also been reflected in my own life.

In the end, my son did not "make an interesting chapter" in my book. America deprived us both of that opportunity. He was a loving young man, in search of himself. But death found him first. His role in my life was far too brief, and not a day passes without a thought of him.

My family history began with sadness and ends on a similar note. Prussia no longer exists, but it is not its demise as a political entity that I mourn. It is the fact that few of the people who filled my pages and to whom I am related had a place in my consciousness as I grew to adulthood. I did not know of my ancestors; I was not aware of their accomplishments, their contributions to history, their sufferings, or their joys. In recalling their lives as well as my own, I hope I have done justice to all.

Chapel Hill, North Carolina
May 10, 2021

Sources

1. United States Holocaust Memorial Museum, Timeline of Events, www.ushmm.org
2. Wikipedia, "Pskov," last modified April 16, 2021.
3. Wikipedia, "History of Latvia," last modified April 12, 2021.
4. Wikipedia, "Johann Wolfgang von Goethe," last modified May 7, 2021.
5. Wikipedia, "Paleolinguistics," last modified March 3, 2021.
6. Wikipedia, "National Liberalism," last modified March, 2021.
7. Wikipedia, "War Merit Cross," last modified April, 2021.
8. Wikipedia, "Anthroposophy," last modified March, 2021.
9. Richard Garner, "The Big Question: Who Was Rudolf Steiner and what were his revolutionary ideas?" *The Independent*: January 24, 2007, 1.
10. Garner, "The Big Question," 2.
11. Wikipedia, "Anthroposophy," last modified May 11, 2021, 9.
12. Wikipedia, "Anthroposophy," last modified May11, 2021, 9.
13. Wikiwand, "Anthroposophy," last modified April, 2021.
14. Wikipedia, "Brandenburg an der Havel," last modified May, 2021.
15. Siarchiv.de: Regionales Personenlexicon zum Nationalismus in den Altkreisen Siegen & Wittgenstein, (Personal Files, German and translated by author), July 2014.
16. Siarchiv.de (Personal Files), July 2014.
17. Wikipedia, "Welfare State Germany," last edited May 6, 2021.
18. Pierre Broue, *The German Revolution* (Chicago, Illinois: HaymarketBooks, 2006), 96.
19. Libcom.org, "Working class activity and councils-Germany 1918-1923 - Peter Rachleff, Nov. 8, 2009, 1.

20. Pierre Broue, *The German Revolution* (Chicago, Illinois: HaymarketBooks, 2006), 96.

21. Pierre Broue, The German Revolution (Chicago, Illinois: HaymarketBooks, 2006), 96.

22. A. J. Ryder, *"Twentieth Century Germany: From Bismarck to Brandt,"* (New York: Columbia University Press, 1973), 186.

23. A. J. Ryder, 186.

24. A. J. Ryder, 186.

25. Ledebour's Trial, Theodor Liebknecht's Defense—Personal Files

26. MR Online, "The League Against Imperialism (1927-37): An early attempt at global anti-colonial unity," John Riddell, July 20, 2018.

27. www.historyguide.org. On the suppressed Testament of Lenin, "The Testament of Lenin" Last modified April 13, 2012.

28. Wikipedia, "Bernard Leach," last modified March, 2021.

29. Bernard Leach, *A Potter's Book*, (Great Britain: Transatlantic Arts Inc. 1970), 11.

30. History News Network, George Washington University, Columbia College of Arts and Sciences, "The Grosse Pointe Point System," William Thompson, July, 2003.

31. Wikipedia, "Werner Hegemann," last modified December, 2020, 2.

32. Wikipedia, Werner Hegemann, Biography, last edited December, 2020.

33. Wikipedia, "Order of Merit of the Federal Republic of Germany," last modified February 9, 2021.

Acknowledgments

I thank my husband for all his encouragement and support during my frequent "mental absences" while writing my family history. He has happily accompanied me to the places of my childhood and shared my pleasure in reliving the past.

To my cousin Christine Lougheed, I owe eternal gratitude for the many hours she spent translating my father's Norwegian letters. Without her, there would only be half a story.

Enormous gratitude goes to Mig Hayes, who was always ready to assist with computer-related problems.

And a very big thank-you to my friends who believed that this was a tale worth telling.

List of Family Members and
Their Relation to the Author

Paternal Relatives

Jakob Heinrich von Wilm: Father of Marie von Wilm, my great-great-grandfather

Marie von Wilm: Mother of Rudolf, Katharina, Else, and Gertrud, my great-grandmother

Dr. Otto Schrader: Husband of Marie von Wilm, father of Rudolf, Katharina, Else, and Gertrud, my great-grandfather

Katharina (Kaethe) Schrader: Daughter of Otto Schrader and Marie von Wilm, wife of Walther Hesse, my grandmother

Walther Hesse: Husband of Katharina Schrader, brother of Alice, my grandfather

Moritz Hesse: Father of Walther and Alice Hesse, my great-grandfather

Marie Pesch: Wife of Moritz, mother of Walther and Alice Hesse, my great-grandmother

Wolfgang Hesse: Son of Walther and Katharina Hesse, my father

Helga Scholze: Wolfgang Hesse's first wife, my birth mother

Vivi Olaussen: Wolfgang Hesse's fiancée, mother of Rolf

Rolf Olaussen Hesse: Son of Vivi and Wolfgang, my half-brother

Gabriele Hesse Miniter: Daughter of Wolfgang Hesse and Helga Scholze, me

Martha and Arthur Pohl: My foster parents

Waltraud Reuter: Second wife of Wolfgang Hesse, mother of Gisela and Marion, my stepmother

Gisela Hesse: Daughter of Wolfgang Hesse and Waltraud Reuter, my half-sister

Marion Hesse: Daughter of Wolfgang Hesse and Waltraud Reuter, my half-sister

Maternal Relatives

Paul Scholze: Grandfather

Martha Scholze: Grandmother

Helga (Scholze Hesse) Smythe: My mother, and mother of Klaudia and Nicola

Frank Scholze: Brother of Helga, my uncle

Nicola Smythe: Daughter of Helga (Scholze Hesse) Smythe, my half-sister

Klaudia Friedrich: Daughter of Helga Scholze and unknown father, my half-sister

The Extended Family

Alice Hesse von Pechmann: Daughter of Moritz and Maria Hesse, sister of Walther Hesse, first wife of Werner Hegemann, second wife of Baron Guenther von Pechmann, my great-aunt

Guenther von Pechmann: Second husband of Alice Hesse, (Hegemann) Great Uncle

Gabriele and Beatrix von Pechmann: Granddaughters of Guenther and Alice, my second cousins

Lightning Source UK Ltd.
Milton Keynes UK
UKHW010739110621
385337UK00001B/21